M000107262

Northern Flavours

Food from Finland

Anna-Maija Tanttu

Northern Flavours

Food from Finland

Helsingissä Kustannusosakeyhtiö Otava

Second edition

Translated by Malcolm Hicks

Lay-out by Maikki Rantala Praxis Ltd

Printed by Otava Book Printing Ltd, Keuruu Finland 2011

ISBN: 978-951-1-20754-2

Contents

Preface

Four seasons and four reasons!

Welcome to join me on a gastronomic adventure in Finland – to peep into Finnish kitchens, visit shops and markets and sample the delicacies on offer at manor houses and restaurants throughout the country. We shall also have a chance to taste foods gathered from nature.

The Finnish gastronomic year is full of new expectations, and although the spring, summer and autumn are the richest times of the year, there are still some good things to look out for in the cold winter season as well.

Finnish cookery is an integral part of European cookery, as our customs in this respect have been greatly influenced by food preferences in neighbouring countries, mainly Sweden in the west and Russia in the east. Our basic food is a blend of peasant fare and the eating habits of the great manor houses, suitably spiced with northern flavours from Lapland and a tinge of Central European cuisine introduced by the master chefs who came here via St. Petersburg. Nowadays one major factor of significance that has turned so many aspects of our lives upside down is the European Union, in addition to which the increase in overseas travel and its extension to the far corners of the earth have made their own contribution to what the Finns choose to eat.

People in Finland can eat well and enjoy a wide variety of food if they so desire. Virtually anything is available; it's all a matter of choice. The most genuine tastes and homely foods can be found in our market places and market halls. These are the real meeting

 The scent of dill is a common feature of Finnish summer dishes.

places for people with culinary interests, and our home-made food is still influenced by traditional and local customs.

School and works canteen meals are served on common sense principles and are a blend of what is healthy and what is enjoyable. They are a part of the Finnish food strategy. Meanwhile, there is a desire to revive traditional dishes and convert many forgotten recipes into branded products. Gastronomic experiences can be had around the buffet tables of manor house restaurants and at local food fairs throughout the country.

The kitchens of the best restaurants are committed to following the latest trends, of course, and the chefs, in their search for taste, quality and freshness, are apt to favour local produce and convert the traditional foods as if by magic into something different in both looks and flavour. The most recent trend is "modern Scandinavian cuisine". One especially pleasing thing is that the Michelin restaurant guide has at last discovered Finland.

This book provides a selection of Finnish recipes, for home-made food, traditional dishes and restaurant specialities, including suggested menus for the various seasons of the year that can be produced relatively easily at home.

I hope they will convince you that a voyage of discovery into the world of Finnish food is well worth the trouble!

Tapiola, 15th March 2007

Anna-Maija Tanttu

Symbols of the Finnish Gastronomic World

Rye bread, butter, milk and soured milk? Potatoes? *Kalakukko* and *mämmi*? *Pulla*? Or "sauna sausage", which is advertised as the ultimate joy for the Finns? The symbols of our eating habits have changed as the years have gone by and as the spread of information, marketing, travel and attention to the health implications of what we eat have all increased. Nowadays pleasure and the promotion of health go hand in hand. Finnish people know how to eat light, healthy meals and to look critically at what is on their plate, on the "eat properly and feel good" principle. At the same time we are prepared nowadays for both home-made and international foods. Suitably adapted to Finnish conditions, pizza has become one of our favourite

meals, especially since a forerunner of it can be found in our own traditions, in the form of the flat, unleavened *rieska* bread. Another obvious alternative that has emerged in recent times is organic food, and locally produced food is also much sought-after.

Finnish people who travel a lot or who live abroad are said to hanker after rye bread, crispbread, cured herring, sauna sausage *(lenkkimakkara)* with mustard, pea soup *(hernekeitto)* and pancake *(pannukakku)*, little pancakes *(ohukaiset)* with jam on, the *pulla* coffee buns and cold milk, and other things that arouse precious memories of home are black pudding, Karelian pasties with egg butter, *kalakukko*, *mämmi*, liquorice and sal ammoniac pastilles, or *salmiakki*. Similar thoughts are also entertained, of course, by chefs who are specialized in Finnish foods when they have to arrange their favourite dishes in order of preference: is it to be cabbage rolls stuffed with lamb, fried fillets of perch with new potatoes, smoked whitefish with chanterelle sauce, Karelian pasties with egg butter, old-fashioned meat balls or palepork sausage (*siskonmakkara*) soup?

Great value is placed on the Finnish traditional foods, and various projects have been undertaken to revive and perpetuate them. There is the Finnfood project aimed at promoting the use of Finnish raw materials in cooking, the use of a Blue Swan mark on packagings to indicate that at least 50% of the ingredients were produced in Finland, and the corresponding badge issued to restaurants that undertake to use only Finnish meat, milk, eggs and related products in preparing dishes whose origins are indicated. A similar joint project, Skärgårdssmak, "A Taste of the Archipelago", exists to promote the coastal food traditions common to Finland and Sweden.

Rye bread is a tradition.

The Culinary Merger of the Century

Lightly salted (*gravad*) whitefish (lavaret) with dill and rosé pepper.

Given that Finland was a part of the kingdom of Sweden for centuries and subject to Russian rule for over a hundred years, both countries have had a considerable influence on Finnish food. This meeting of cultures has allowed a new international, and above all European, culinary tradition to develop, an original tradition that keeps up with the times and is prepared to adopt new influences from different countries and from its own peasant and manor house customs. The foundation for its cuisine nevertheless consists of the ingredients provided by nature.

A few ingredients from the west, a few from the east and some additions from Lapland and the archipelago; nor is Finland even today by any means slow to adopt exotic tastes and ideas taken from alien cultures as parts of its national diet – in fact we are quite skilful at it. Indeed, Finnish food has become far more fun and far more colourful in recent times as people have ventured to give it a new, happy and youthful image.

Adopted from Swedish cooking

A large proportion of our everyday foods originate from our western neighbour, Sweden. Many of the great manor houses of South-Western Finland, Uusimaa and Häme served in their day as communicators of European cooking and eating habits, establishing kitchen gardens of their own on the Swedish model and learning to grow apple trees, currant bushes, rhubarb and horseradish. The use of vegetables spread via the servants who used to work in these gardens and caught on with ordinary people. The first cookery books in Finland were ones that had been translated from Swedish.

Fresh-salted whitefish or salmon

for each kg of fish fillets:
2 tbsp coarse sea salt
1/4–1/2 tbsp sugar
1 tsp coarsely ground white pepper
a few sprigs of dill

Clean and fillet the fish, but do not skin them. Place one of the fillets skin-side down in a dish and sprinkle with a mixture of salt, sugar and white pepper. Sprinkle with chopped dill, both the leaves and the stems.

Place another fillet skin-side up on top of the first. Sprinkle the rest of the salt mixture and dill on this. Cover with cling film and place a suitable weight on top. Keep in a cold place for a day.

Scrape the spices off the surface and slice thinly. Serve with boiled potatoes (preferably new potatoes) and chopped dill.

The Russian tradition

The most tangible influence on Finnish food has nevertheless been exercised by Russia, for there are a host of pies, mushroom dishes, dark breads and numerous other foods and delicate eating habits that the Finns have adopted from the Russians and have learned to appreciate and love. These delicacies are usually prepared according to traditional recipes. Our everyday foods include many features that are of Russian origin, including pickled cucumbers, sauerkraut, cabbage and borsch soups, preserved mushrooms, stroganoff and blinis served with roe and herring or with mushroom salad, frequently accompanied by a dash of *smetana*, an ancient form of full-flavoured soured cream that is an essential element in Russian cuisine. One delicious and highly popular hors d'oeuvres is strips of pickled cucumber topped with honey and *smetana*.

Our sweet desserts made of quark form a chapter of their own. Known in Russian as *tvorog*, which means milk soured in the oven, quark is scarcely ever made at home nowadays but is usually bought unflavoured from the shops. A new departure in recent times has also been flavoured quark. Quark is used to lighten desserts and pastry and to make pies and tarts, etc. It is easy to imagine when eating Finnish quark pastries that these must have been the origin of American cheesecake.

Flavours from elsewhere in the world

The Finns of today have discovered many new favourite foods in Europe and America and have copied them or adapted them to the Finnish palate. When the Finns fell for the hamburger, they developed their own version in which the meat and

Strips of pickled cucumber served with honey and smetana is a Russian-style starter.

Pickled cucumbers, honey and smetana

A delicious combination that is popular as a starter, especially in Russian-style restaurants.

(FOR TWO PERSONS)

1–2 pickled cucumbers/person
about 1 dl liquid honey
1 dl smetana, or sour cream

Cut the cucumbers into segments lengthwise and serve with the honey and smetana, all in separate dishes.

Take some slices of cucumber onto your plate, pour a little honey on them and top with a dash of smetana. Eat them with your fingers or with a knife and fork.

lettuce was put into a rye bread roll. Likewise many households in eastern Finland have a pasta machine, but instead of using it to churn out sheets of lasagne or strips of tagliatelli, they have found it ideal for making the crusts for their Karelian pasties. One of the very first culinary merger experiments, in the 1960s, was the *kapitsa*, a Karelian pasty disguised as a pizza by topping it off with a mixture of tomato, cheese and oregano. Now, fifty years later, there are many Finns who would regard pizza or burgers as their favourite foods, although there is still a good deal of support for traditional dishes such as fried vendace, Baltic herrings or *pyttipannu*. The favourite among adults who frequent restaurants still seems to be pepper steak!

Membership of the European Union and the unlimited availability of imported foodstuffs has played havoc with our old eating customs. The Finns of today are quite at home cooking pasta, making sauces to go on it, and eating mozzarella cheese, parma ham and breasts of duck. They also eat exotic fruits and with the boom in travel to the Far East, have acquired a liking for Asian foods.

The shops offer their customers Christmas all year round, although few people seriously want to buy new potatoes or fresh garden strawberries in the depths of winter. The true Finns are content to live in harmony with the seasons, wait patiently for the right foods to appear on the market and concentrate on these. They are also anxious to observe the traditions of their own area, even if they no longer take these traditional foods so deadly seriously as they used to. Each district has its own dishes, forms of bread and species of fish which it favours, however, just as the various provinces have their own special flowers, birds and even rocks.

The Pick of Regional Dishes

The most authentic, ancient Finnish flavours are those to be found in the traditional dishes, and although some of these have been forgotten in the meantime, efforts are being made to revive them and develop them to suit the modern-day palate. Again a merger of some sort has been taking place.

It may be hard to imagine the attraction of oat kissel, slaughterer's soup or blood pancakes – exotic rarities even for Finnish people, but it may be as well to forget your prejudices and try these old dishes if they come your way. It is also fun to take part in various events connected with food, whether they be rituals, feasts, markets and tastings, meals at manor houses or medieval banquets in the proper surroundings, such as Turku Castle or the castle of Hämeenlinna.

Our tour of the regions, during which we will pick out a few notable dishes from each, will begin on the Åland Islands.

Åland being a group of islands in the sea area between Finland and Sweden, it is natural to begin by sampling its fish dishes: Baltic herrings baked in the oven, for instance, or pike in one form or another. The local bread, which is black and somewhat sweet, with a strong taste of malt, and comes in flat loaves, is also particularly good with herring dishes. For dessert it is imperative to try Åland pancakes, which have semolina or rice in their dough and are served with strawberry or raspberry jam. More recent novelties include pickled onions, sold in glass jars, which are especially suitable on meat, and *Ålvados*, a fortified wine made of Åland apples, Finland's equivalent of Calvados.

Åland oven pancake

1 litre milk

1 dl pudding rice or semolina

2 eggs

1 dl sugar

1 dl plain flour

1/2 tsp salt

a little ground cardamom

Bring the milk to the boil and whisk in the rice or semolina. Cook for 20 minutes to make a porridge. Cool. Whisk the eggs and sugar and add them to the porridge. Stir in the flour, salt and cardamom.

Grease an oven tray. Pour in the batter and bake the pancake in a hot oven, 225–250°C, until golden brown.

Serve with jam and whipped cream.

In Varsinais-Suomi, Southwestern Finland, a good buffet table will always include *sallatti* and *piimäjuusto*, soured milk cheese. Great use is made on the coast of sprats, *vaspuukeja*, which are preserved in glass jars, layered with allspice, onions and bay leaves in a salt and sugar marinade. Tripe and raisin sausages are a reminder of the days when the cattle were mainly slaughtered in the autumn. One should not turn one's nose up at beer gruel, *kaljavelli*, either, as this sweet soup flavoured with gingerbread spices makes a wonderful dessert. Among the local drinks the blackcurrant leaf cordial prepared at the manor house of Louhisaari is known throughout the country. All in all, the outstanding features of the food of Southern Finland are the influences adopted from elsewhere, and particularly their international character. Turku area delights its visitors with the

The Baltic herring is a little fish with a great taste.

first new potatoes in Finland each spring, and later the first outdoor strawberries. The city is also famous for its sweet mustard and its excellent restaurants.

Satakunta is another area that is famous for its fish dishes, as much for whitefish, or lavaret, as for Baltic herring. This is the home of salted whitefish, whitefish soup and whitefish cooked in the glow of an open fire. Cut in half, flattened and nailed to a wooden board, this is sometimes known as "crucified whitefish". The idea is, of course, that it should cook in the glow from the fire without the flames actually touching it. This is also the home of Baltic herring bread and of a special barley bread, *kakko*, that is baked in a stone oven. Goat's cheese is popular here, and the bakeries of Eura are famous for their ring cookies, *rinkelit*, and those of Pori for their cognac cookies, or *plarit*.

The lamprey is neither a fish nor a snake but a cyclostome, a primitive animal with a round, open mouth that can be caught with cages. Satakunta is a good area for lampreys, which can be enjoyed from August onwards each year. After salting, they are baked over the hot embers of a fire until tender and then sold at markets or in stalls by the roadside. The traditional food in Rauma is *lapskaus*, a potato and meat hash.

The province of Pohjanmaa, Ostrobothnia, has many typical dishes based on catches from the open sea and archipelago and the rich harvests from the fields. Fish, especially Baltic herring, is eaten a great deal and is prepared in a wide variety of ways: herring caviar, herrings in a juniper berry marinade, and herrings tartare made of fresh, uncooked fish. In Sundom they smoke herrings in an unusual way, hanging them vertically in the smoke box from a rod pushed through the eyes.

The flat white "bread cheese", *leipäjuusto*, with its brown patches is known all over the country, but its home is in Ostrobothnia, where it served at one time as a means of storing milk in cheese form for the winter or for taking on a journey. The more cheeses you could see through the attic window of a house, the wealthier the family was. It is also an old custom to break the cheese into small pieces and drop it into one's coffee.

Many sweet tastes in food have come from the west, across the Gulf of Bothnia, including the liking for sweet bread, the best-known of which is from Malax. Also in the Swedish-speaking part of Ostrobothnia is the village of Stundars, nowadays a living museum, where feasts are arranged in summer at which they serve meat soup with wheat flour dumplings.

Bread cheese *(leipäjuusto)* is made with rennet. Eat it just as it is or heated and topped with berries.

Ostrobothnia is part of the "hard bread" area of Finland, where the custom was to bake flat, circular loaves with a hole in the middle, *reikäleipä*, and hang them on rails near the kitchen ceiling to dry. Also round, but anything but hard are the flat unleaved loaves baked in this area, *rieska*, which can even contain mashed turnip.

The food of Northern Ostrobothnia has been influenced by Lapland customs, while the particular delicacy of the coastal areas in the north is sea buckthorn berries, for which a special tool is required for picking the berries from the spiny bushes. When crushed, these berries yield a purée and a juice that are both very rich in vitamin C.

One essential place to visit in autumn is the stretch of rapids on the Tornio River known as Kukkolankoski, where they use long-handled hoop nets to catch whitefish, which are then mounted lengthways on sticks and cooked over an open fire.

Ostrobothnian "bread cheese" *(leipäjuusto)* with cream and jam

Cut the bread cheese into suitable portions and place them in a greased oven dish. Add enough thick cream to just cover the pieces of cheese. Sprinkle with sugar and cinnamon.

Heat in a 250°C oven for about 5 minutes. Serve with cold cloudberry, raspberry, redcurrant or blackcurrant jam.

The special flavour comes from the salt water into which they are plunged after cooking.

The local fish of Kainuu, the smelt, can be enjoyed at its best at the carnivals held during its spawning time in spring, while the delicacy of the gentry is a clear whitefish soup. The region is famous for its local pies, or *rönttöset*, filled with potato or berries. The revival of the old tar-making customs has led to its use in cookery as well, so that people have learned to spread tar syrup on their bread cheese in the manner of honey, add tar jelly to meat dishes and enjoy at other times the latest invention for Kainuu, tar chocolates.

The speciality of the north-east of the country, Koillismaa, is the small vendace known as the "wise old man of Kitka", after the lake in which they are traditionally caught. These are eaten either salted or stewed in a pot with pork. Kuusamo is also known for its smoked cheeses.

The vendace, *muikku*, is known best as the provincial fish of Savo, however, where it is an essential part of both the festive and everyday diet. The delicacy to beat all delicacies is a plate of vendace crisply fried on a cast-iron pan over an open fire, while another favourite is *rantakala*, a soup of freshly caught vendace with onions and potatoes cooked in a large cauldron. Kuopio, the capital city of Savo, is the place for fish pies, *kalakukko*, made of a rye bread crust with vendace, perch, rainbow trout or burbot interleaved with layers of pork inside and baked for sufficient time that the bones are as soft as in a tin of sardines. Another traditional dish, *tirripaisti*, also calls for strips of belly pork, which are fried until crisp and then cooked over a low heat. A local dessert is *rättänä*, similarly made with a rye crust but filled with a sweet bilberry mixture.

These "whitefish on sticks" will be plunged into salt water when they are done.

The traditional Karelian pasties have now spread all over Finland. They are usually filled with boiled rice or barley, but mashed potato or puréed vegetables can also be used.

Karelian pasties *(karjalanpiirakat)*

(FOR 12–14 PASTIES)

1 dl water
1/2–1 tsp salt
about 2 dl rye flour
1/2 dl plain flour
+ some extra flour

for the filling:

1 litre milk
2 dl uncooked pudding rice
salt

to moisten:

melted butter or butter and water

Add the flour and salt to the water and mix into a solid, compact dough.

Heat the milk and add the rice. Simmer for at least 20 minutes to make a thick porridge. Season with salt.

Form the dough into a bar and divide into 12–14 or more parts.

Roll into balls and flatten into cakes.

Sprinkle the baking surface and the rolling pin with rye flour.

Roll the cakes into thin sheets with the rolling pin, thin enough "to see seven churches through it", as the saying goes.

Spread some of the filling on each sheet, turn the edges in about a centimetre over the filling and press them into place.

Put the pasties onto an oven tray and bake in the hottest possible oven for a couple of minutes. The pasties are ready when the bottom is slightly browned and the rice filling has a few brown patches on it.

Brush the pasties well with melted butter or a mixture of butter and water.

Place them in a bowl with greaseproof paper between them and cover with a towel to soften the crusts.

Serve warm with egg butter.

Egg butter *(munavoi)*

150 g butter
2 hard-boiled eggs

Soften and cream the butter.

Finely chop the eggs and mix with the butter to a spreading consistency.

For a modern version, use cottage cheese instead of hard-boiled eggs.

The *ryynirieska* of the Pieksämäki area of Southern Savo is a tasty bread made of pearl barley and often served with a mixture of egg and butter.

Karelian pasties, *karjalanpiirakat*, and Karelian stew, *karjalanpaisti*, are the gastronomic delights that **Pohjois-Karjala**, Northern Karelia, has given to the rest of Finland. The wonderfully fragrant stew contains layers of pork, beef and lamb together with liver and kidney. Northern Karelia is renowned for its dishes that are baked or stewed in the oven, and even the homes of the young people of today are filled with the aroma of meat dishes cooking slowly in the oven, especially at weekends.

This is also an area for pies, filled with vendace or other fish or else swede, but here they are flatter and lighter in colour than those of Savo. Breakfast often includes barley porridge cooked in the oven and eaten with a fruit soup made from berries.

It is at Lemi in **Etelä-Karjala**, Southern Karelia, that we find one of Finland's "seven wonders", *säräpaisti*, roast lamb cooked in a wooden tray with potatoes and root vegetables and covered to cook slowly until tastily tender right through. The best way of getting to taste this in a genuine atmosphere is to join an organized group or arrange for a private meal at the local restaurant, or *säräpirtti*, that specializes in it.

A good memento to bring back from the market is a giant-sized Vyborg ring bun, *Viipurin rinkeli*, made of a water-based wheat dough and spiced with nutmeg. Another thing to buy at the market in Lappeenranta is a new form of meat pie, known as "Hydrogen and Atom", which is filled with either boiled or smoked ham and a boiled egg and deep-fried in fat.

Keski-Suomi, Central Finland, is an area in which influences from different parts of the country meet. Almost all the types of bread known in Finland can be found there, for instance, although the oldest is an unleavened barley bread, *ohrarieska*, often with soured milk added to the dough on more festive occasions and with pearl barley, pre-soaked in the liquid, as well as flour. Along with Häme, this province is also one of the main areas of the country for *talkkuna*, a flour made of roasted grain, often with a slight tang of smoke to it. The variety that contains mainly oats is the most tasty in many people's opinion, but barley and various mixtures of grain with peas are also used. Fish is traditionally served at every meal, and *patakukko*, fish pie made in a dish, *rantakala, suutarinpaisti* and *säynemureke*, minced ide loaf, are other fish dishes that have risen in popularity in the area.

In **Häme** it is common to make cheese with sour milk or egg and milk in a mould, giving it a beautiful golden colour on the outside by baking it quickly in a hot oven. The moist egg cheese is often to be found in buffets, as is meat aspic, or *aladobi*. Other "musts" in this area are *perunalaatikko*, sweetened mashed potato baked in the oven, and a salad known as *rosolli* made of boiled beetroot, potatoes and other root vegetables. The salted fish eaten in this area used to be local, either bream or roach, but nowadays rainbow trout is often used. The local forms of bread are barley bread, *ohrarievä*, malt bread, *varikoinen*, and potato bread, and the traditional drink is home-brewed beer, or on festive occasions the alcoholic equivalent of this, the cloudy brew called *sahti*. Prune kissel is popular as a dessert, while an older and less common dessert nowadays is a porridge made of rye flour and lingonberries baked in the oven. *Mustamakkara*, black pudding, is even a part of the hotel breakfast in Tampere, but you can also buy it in the market hall, at the factory where it is made and, especially at night, in kiosks along the streets. It is at its best when accompanied by lingonberry sauce and milk or soured milk.

The food of Kymenlaakso, the Kymi Valley, has always been fairly cosmopolitan, being influenced particularly by the Russians who had their villas there in earlier times. The appearance of wild mushrooms on the Finns' dining tables can largely be attributed to this influence, for instance. This is another area where there is plenty of fish to be had, and particular delicacies are Baltic herrings baked over hot embers, herring rolls, *silakkaserpa* and salted ide.

Uusimaa, the province in which the capital, Helsinki, is situated, is a melting pot for culinary traditions. It is difficult to find really traditional foods that are specific to this area, but some local features can be seen in the context of home cooking or buffet meals. Baltic herrings, *silakat*, are eaten mainly baked on hot embers or smoked, or else baked in a casserole in the oven or prepared in various sauces as an hors d'oeuvres. Crisply fried Baltic herrings can be found even in the best restaurants at lunchtime, and some have based their reputation on this dish. The speciality of the parish of Inkoo is potato porridge, and the same area's rarity, potato sausage, is also worth trying if you have the chance. The constant stream of migration within the country has greatly affected eating habits in recent times, and not even the people of Helsinki can be said to have any traditional foods any longer, unless you count boiled pike with egg sauce as such, or perhaps potatoes with sausage sauce, or even sausage soup!

Salmon, Baltic herrings, whitefish or other fish, minced meat, mushrooms or even vegetables can be interleaved with layers of potato to produce a tasty casserole (see the recipe for salmon and potato casserole, p. 66).

The magic of Lapland

Lapland is the northernmost province of Finland and covers about 30% of the country's area. With its "magic nights" and Aurora Borealis, its barren landscapes and its reindeer, it is an exotic holiday and travel destination for many Finns as well as for visitors from abroad. The first snow often falls there in September and the skiing season can last till May Day. There is a period around Christmas when the sun does not rise at all, and a corresponding period around midsummer when it never sets.

When people speak of Lapland they often conjure up romantic images of Lapps living in tents and tending reindeer, but although quite a lot of people do make their living from reindeer herding. The main source of livelihood in Lapland these days is nevertheless tourism.

One can become carried away with Lapland in very many ways. One successful and well organized weekend spent there may be enough to sow the seed of a romance that will bring you back there again and again, for hiking in the summer, for the autumn colours or for the winter skiing. The atmosphere is at its most authentic when you are sitting in a Lapp tent or beside an open fire, sipping coffee from the traditional wooden cup, or *kuksa*. It is there, eating and drinking in the midst of nature, that you can savour the centuries-old nomadic way of life. There is a whole network of shelters and huts available for hikers to spend the night in, and even more places for lighting fires on the hiking routes.

As a holiday destination Lapland has a wealth of new experiences to offer: the midnight sun, expeditions by boat or canoe, hiking trips, or the life of the luxury skiing resorts with their enjoyable nightlife. Or if you prefer, there is the peace and solitude of a private holiday cottage. The main occupations in winter-time are skiing, riding on dog sleighs, fishing through the ice or snowmobile safaris.

Rides in a reindeer or dog sleigh are part of the fun of Lapland in winter.

Children usually want to go to the land of Santa Claus and to make a fuss of the reindeer that pull Santa's sleigh and carry his presents. If you don't happen to see a herd of reindeer on the road, you can be sure of seeing some in paddocks behind the houses.

Gastronomically, Lapland had been reached by a wave of new ingredients, imaginative ideas and international trends. Apart from classics such as reindeer hash, salmon soup and cloudberries on "bread cheese", there are all manner of novelties to try: *kätkätykset*, or small delicacies eaten rather in a style of tapas, for instance, or reindeer leg chops cooked until soft in a spicy broth. The young chefs in the "fine dining" restaurants are not short of good ingredients, as there is plenty to choose from: willow grouse, fish such as perch, arctic char, trout, burbot and whitefish from the mountain streams and lakes, wild mushrooms and berries. Reindeer tartare can be made with lightly salted or smoked meat, one traditional plant that has been rediscovered is garden angelica (*Angelica archangelica*), which grows wild in Lapland, and the most unexpected newcomer is the Kamchatka crab, or king crab, a giant species from Russia that is appreciated throughout the world and has now established itself on the Arctic Ocean coast of Norway and has become a gastronomic speciality in Finnish Lapland as well.

The gastronomic world of Lappi, Lapland, is an exotic one even for the Finns. Whitefish, salmon, reindeer and willow grouse are held in high esteem, and many a book has been written about them. These northern delicacies are all at their best served with the small, almond-shaped *puikula* potatoes that grow in Lapland. The easiest way of savouring reindeer meat, however, is to shave thin slices off a lump of dried meat with a knife and eat them just like that. It is also from dried meat that the traditional reindeer soup is made.

Dried reindeer meat goes well with coffee made over an open fire in Lapland.

Springtime – Great Expectations

Spring is the time when nature awakens once again, the migratory birds return to their nesting areas and the new leaf buds burst on the deciduous trees. The wood anemone and hepatica begin to flower in the south of Finland and the tulips and narcissus open up in the gardens and yards, while in the north the snow gleams in the sun and the skiing season continues until around the beginning of May.

It is not only the birds that migrate, however, for many people do so as well. This is the beginning of the summer cottage season. The Finns lay much store by their summer cottages, regarding them almost as something sacred, to be secretly longed for, and the sunny spring days are just the time for arousing your cottage from its winter slumbers and holding the first barbeques in the yard or on the terrace. Many people nowadays have a small gazebo in their yard for enjoying their barbeque in.

This is the time for raking up the leaves in the garden and for repainting work in the boatyards. The first rays of the sun soon tempt the open-air restaurants to open up. It is time to take one's first sips of beer on an outdoor veranda, or make one's first visit to the ice cream kiosk.

Easter – a spring festival

The highlight of the spring season is Easter. The festive fare of the Orthodox Church that has come to us from the east has found its way onto many Finnish dining tables, and without any especially religious thoughts in mind the Finns are now happy to eat the foods that in earlier times were prohibited during Lent. Grass seed is sown on plates in good time to

Previous spread:
The wood anemone (*Anemone nemorosa*) is one of the early signs of spring.

Pussy willows and daffodils symbolize Easter.

A spring menu

- Nettle soup
- Fried fillets of perch with a chopped false morel sauce, cucumber and radish salad
- Rhubarb kissel

grow ready for Easter, and vases are filled with yellow Easter lilies and pussy-willows. Green and yellow are the colours of the day. The children paint and decorate Easter eggs, and the more skilful adults have developed this into an art form, embellishing them with pearls, imitation jewelstones and ribbons in the style of the world-famous goldsmith Fabergé in his time.

One of the delights of Easter in Finland is the Mignon egg, a real eggshell filled with the finest nougat chocolate. The customary meat is roast lamb, and the typical dessert is either *mämmi* or *pasha*, a sweet creamy pudding made of quark that is spread on slices of a sweet, spicy bread known as *kulitsa*. An alternative is *baba*, an elaborately decorated cake flavoured with rum or punch that is usually bought ready made from a baker's.

Mämmi

This chocolate-brown paste made from rye flour is a healthy and very traditional Easter food, and was also regarded at one time as a Lenten food, being particularly associated with Good Friday, when one was not expected to indulge in especially tasty food nor to waste time on cooking. This porridge-like dish was a good solution, as it is sweet-tasting and is usually eaten cold.

Nowadays *mämmi* is more of a dessert to be eaten at Easter itself, and has its detractors as well as its admirers. It is prepared industrially throughout the country, often in small bakeries, but few people make it at home any longer. It is dark brown in colour and smells and tastes of malt and orange, with a whiff of liquorice to it as well. The main ingredients are rye flour, rye malt and water. Our present-day "organic" *mämmi* has no other sweeteners, but it is normal to add syrup or sugar and Seville orange peel.

The traditional Easter foods include *mämmi*, the creamy dessert known as *pascha*, a sweet bread called *kulitsa* and red-painted eggs. In the foreground are spoon biscuits and a Mignon egg, a real eggshell filled with fine chocolate.

An Easter menu

- Eggs filled with roe and herring
- Roast lamb basted with coffee, potato au gratin and Brussels sprouts
- Mämmi, pasha or kulitsa

Roast lamb basted with coffee
(kahvilammas)

2 1/2 kg joint of lamb for roasting
2 cloves of garlic
salt
ground black pepper
Dijon mustard
about 1/2 litre strong coffee
2–4 dl whipping cream
(2 tbsp gin or port wine)
for the roasting dish:
2 whole bulbs of garlic

Take the joint of meat out into room temperature a couple of hours before roasting. Split the cloves of garlic and rub them into the meat all over. Dab the surface with salt and black pepper.

Place the joint on a deep oven tray or in a suitably large dish. Spread the mustard on the joint with a pastry brush or knife. Heat the oven to 225°C. Roast the meat until it is nicely browned on the surface and the mustard has formed a hard crust. In the meantime, make the strong coffee and mix a couple of decilitres of cream into it. Reduce the oven temperature to 175°C and baste the meat with two or three spoonfuls of this creamy coffee. Repeat this every 15 minutes, using the coffee that has drained down into the oven tray or dish as well. Make sure that there is always some coffee in the tray or dish. The more you baste the meat with coffee, the better it will taste. If you wish, you can add gin or port wine to the coffee after about an hour and continue using this mixture. The meat will still be red in the middle at 71°C, but will be cooked through at an internal temperature of 77°C. If you prefer your roast lamb to be very well done, keep it in the oven for another half hour after this.

When done to your satisfaction, take the joint out of the oven and wrap it in aluminium foil. Sieve the juice remaining in the oven tray or dish into a saucepan and scrape in any tasty scraps of meat or seasoning as well. Bring to the boil, add cream and thicken with cornflour or a mixture of butter and flour.

If you wish, cook a couple of whole bulbs of garlic beside the joint, just like roast potatoes. Peel off their outer skins and put the bulbs in the dish or oven tray. They will take about an hour to cook.

Spoon biscuits
(lusikkaleivät)

200 g butter
1 1/2 dl sugar
2 tsp vanillin
250 g plain flour
1 tsp baking soda
for the filling:
raspberry jam or apple purée

Brown the butter in a clean frying pan. Pour it into a bowl and add the sugar. Mix until the butter is cool, but do not whisk to a foam.

Combine the dry ingredients and add them to the butter mixture.

Press small pieces of dough into the bowl of a teaspoon and turn the spoon-shaped biscuits out onto an oven tray covered with greaseproof paper. Bake at 200°C until light brown. Cool.

Stick the biscuits together in pairs with jam in between. Be careful, because they break easily!

Pasha

5 dl quark

150 g butter

1 dl sugar

2 egg yolks

3/4 dl ground almonds

(1 tbsp chopped candied orange peel)

1 dl chopped raisins

1–2 tsp vanilla sugar

Begin preparing the pasha on the day before you intend to serve it. Spoon the quark into a coffee filter and allow it to drain overnight.

Make sure that the orange peel and raisins are chopped into sufficiently small pieces. Beat the butter and sugar together to a light froth, mix in the egg yolks and then add the rest of the ingredients and stir well. Finally add the quark after it has drained and stir again.

Pasha can be served on its own, as a spread.

If you want to form it into a cone or pyramid, line a suitable mould, e.g. a sieve, with a damp muslin cloth or cheesecloth, spoon the pasha into the mould, turn the edges of the cloth in over the top and place a lightish weight on it. Keep the pasha like this in the fridge for 24 hours, with a plate underneath to catch the excess liquid.

Then turn the pasha out, lift off the cloth and decorate the pasha.

Note:

If you use loose quark you will need to drain it in a sieve beforehand, but the quark sold in pots is ready to use.

Easter cake *(kulitsa)*

1 dl milk

30 g yeast

2 eggs

1 dl sugar

1 tsp salt

100 g soft butter at room temperature

just under 6 dl plain flour

2 1/2 dl raisins

(1 1/4 dl currants)

for decoration:

shelled almonds

Dissolve the fresh yeast in lukewarm milk and add the eggs, salt and sugar.

Fold in the flour and soft butter to produce a dough. Finally add the raisins (and currants).

Allow the dough to rise for about half an hour.

Form the whole dough into a single round cake, allow to rise again, press almonds into its top surface, brush with egg and bake in a 200°C oven for about 35 minutes.

Serve with pasha on your Easter coffee table.

Wild nettles are among the first vegetables to come from nature every spring. They are excellent in soups, creamed, or fried in small pancakes.

Nettle soup

1 litre fresh young nettles
2–3 dl water
2 tbsp butter or margarine
2 tbsp plain flour
6 dl meat or chicken stock, or water containing a stock cube
2 dl thick cream
1/4 tsp grated nutmeg
some hard-boiled eggs

Pick the nettles with gloved hands. Rinse them, put them in a saucepan, add the water and boil for about 5 minutes. Pour the water away. Finely chop the nettles.
Melt the butter or margarine in the saucepan, add the flour, stir and bring to the boil. Add the meat or chicken stock a little at a time, stirring well in between. Add the nettles. Cook for about 5 minutes. Add the nutmeg just before serving. Check for taste, bring to the boil and serve with hard-boiled eggs.

Nettle pancakes

Prepare the nettles as above, finely chop them and stir them into a pancake mixture. Fry as small pancakes.

The mixture is then left to sweeten, served out into cardboard cartons (originally trays made of birch bark), baked in the oven and allowed to cool. It is served with cream and sugar, ice cream or whipped vanilla cream. More recent creations are *mämmi*-flavoured ice cream and a whipped bilberry and *mämmi* shake.

Time for Celebrations

Spring is a time for celebrations. Mother's Day is a family occasion when most mothers manage at least breakfast in bed, on a tray decorated with a rose, but if the family, headed by Father, can't relieve her of her kitchen duties they may well all go out to eat. May Day will certainly mean a visit to a restaurant for many people.

The May Day celebrations, which usually begin the previous evening, are a time of merrymaking for young and old alike. Above all it is the students and workers who celebrate. People will resurrect their student cap, the symbol of having passed the matriculation exam at the end of their school career, and put it on again, regardless of whether it is still a pristine white or has turned yellow with age, and go out to sing light-hearted spring songs with their friends. The whole country is engulfed in a carnival spirit, which even extends to the political festivities arranged by the labour movement.

The most common non-alcoholic drink for the whole family is *sima*, a bubbly, honey-flavoured mead akin to that known from the time of the Vikings, the sweetest versions being those made at home. On the other hand, the traditional May Day food, *tippaleipä*, nests of doughnut mixture extruded into coarse threads and deep-fried, are usually bought from bakeries or patisseries.

Adults drink their May Day toast in sparkling wine or champagne, and begin their lunch with herring garnished with various sauces and washed down with small glasses of ice-cold schnapps.

Soon the ice will have melted on the lakes and rivers, and it will be spawning time for fish such as the perch, pike, rainbow trout, bream, pike-perch, Baltic herring and smelt. A new season of plentiful fishing will be at hand.

Of the mushrooms, the false morels (*Gyromitra esculenta*) appear in spring, and it is exciting to go out and see whether they have come up in their usual places. The first wild plant available for use as a vegetable is the stinging nettle, which can be used in the same way as spinach. Chives sends up its first new shoots at about the same time as the nettles, but you have to wait a little longer for rhubarb.

When the leaves are just opening on the birch trees some of the more inventive among us pick these to make a schnapps of their own, and other people collect the new spruce shoots to make syrup and jelly.

By the end of May it is time to celebrate with the school leavers who have passed their matriculation exams and other young people who have finished their studies or gained their working qualifications.

Spring foods:

false morels, stinging nettles, pike, perch, bream, cucumber and chives

May Day is the time for eating doughnut nests (*tippaleivät*) and drinking mead *(sima)*.

May Day doughnut nests *(tippaleivät)*

2 eggs
2 tsp sugar
1/2 tsp salt
2 dl milk
4 dl plain flour
1/2 tsp vanillin
for frying:
vegetable oil

Mix the eggs and sugar together and beat lightly. Add the other ingredients and stir to a smooth batter.

Put the batter in a paper cone or pastry bag fitted with a nozzle having a small hole.

Cook only one or two doughnuts at a time. Squeeze a thin stream of batter into the hot oil, using a spiral motion so that it forms nest-shaped doughnuts.

Put metal rings in the pot to keep the doughnuts in shape.

When they have turned a golden brown, remove them and drain them on paper towels.

Dust them with icing sugar when cold.

Mead
(sima)

5 litres water

2 lemons

1/4 kg granulated sugar

1/4 kg brown sugar

2 dl treacle or honey

1/4 tsp fresh yeast or a pinch of dried yeast

(1 bottle of beer)

into the bottles:

raisins and sugar

Peel the rind off the lemons (preferably unsprayed – otherwise well scrubbed) with a potato peeler, then remove and discard the white pith and cut both the lemons and their peel into slices.

Place the slices of lemon and peel in a large bowl or bucket with the sugar. Bring the water to the boil and pour it over these ingredients.

Let the mixture cool, and when it is lukewarm, add the yeast, dissolved in a little of the liquid.

Let the mead ferment at room temperature overnight.

Pour through a sieve into bottles. Put a few raisins and a teaspoon of sugar in each bottle before closing it. Keep the bottles at room temperature for a few hours, and then store in a cool place.

The drink is ready to serve in a few days, but is best after a week.

False morel sauce

250 g false morels (Gyromitra esculenta)
pre-processed and preserved or frozen

2–3 tbsp butter

3 dl vegetable stock

2 dl whipping cream

(salt)

(1 tbsp lemon juice or dry sherry)

Strain the mushrooms and cut them into small pieces. Melt the butter, add the mushrooms and cook them in the butter for a moment. Sprinkle with flour, mix this in and gradually add the liquids, stirring all the time. Cook gently for about 20 min. Season.

NB.

Fresh or dried false morels must be pre-processed to remove the poison before use.

For the method of pre-processing, see page 88.

Fried fillets of perch

8–12 fillets of perch

salt, white pepper

plain flour or rye flour

for frying:

butter and a drop of rapeseed oil

Sprinkle the perch fillets on both sides with salt and white pepper, then toss them in the flour. Melt the butter in a frying pan and add a drop of rapeseed oil. When the oil is a golden brown in colour, put the fillets in to fry. Fry on both sides, for 3–4 minutes in all. Serve at once.

Rhubarb jam

1 litre rhubarb, chopped into pieces

250 g granulated or preserving sugar

1/4 dl water

(a vanilla pod)

Put the ingredients in a saucepan. Bring to the boil and cook for about 15 minutes, until the pieces of rhubarb begin to break up and the mixture becomes cloudy and jam-like.

Store in sealed jars or in the deep-freeze.

Rhubarb and strawberry kissel

2–4 sticks rhubarb (about 300 g)

6 dl water

1 dl sugar

about 1/2 litre fresh or frozen strawberries

for thickening:

3 tbsp potato flour + 1/2 dl cold water

Cut the rhubarb into pieces about 2 cm long. Put them in a saucepan, pour the water over them and add the sugar.

Cook gently for about 10 minutes, until the rhubarb begins to break up. Taste, and add sugar if necessary, then take off the heat.

Mix the potato flour into the cold water and add the mixture to the boiled rhubarb in a gentle stream, stirring all the time. Return the saucepan to the heat and bring to the boil, but do not allow to actually boil, as this will thicken the kissel too much.

Cut the strawberries into pieces, place them in the bottom of a serving dish and pour the warm rhubarb kissel on top of them. Stir carefully, sprinkle a little sugar on the surface, cool and serve with milk, cream or vanilla ice cream.

Cucumber and radish salad

1 cucumber

10 radishes

1 tbsp finely chopped dill

1 tbsp finely chopped chives

for the sauce:

1 tbsp lemon juice

4 tbsp rapeseed oil

1/2 tsp salt, black pepper

Peel the cucumber if you wish. Split it in half lengthways and spoon out the seeds.

Slice the radishes.

Mix the ingredients for the sauce. Combine the vegetables with the chopped dill and chives. Stir the sauce and mix it in.

Store in the cold before serving.

Summertime – and White Nights

Summer in Finland is a time for simple, natural gastronomic pleasures, making the most of fresh ingredients. Nature is at its most generous, the nights are light and people are in holiday mood. There are all manner of summer celebrations to gather friends and relatives together. The official holiday month of July, when "Finland closes down" is spent at one's country cottage, boating, walking in the countryside, fishing, pursuing all kinds of hobbies and going to the summer dances.

But the Finnish summer is short: there are just three months in which the whole harvest has to ripen, one item after another, so that there is always something to look forward to. First of all it is new potatoes, which can be eaten with spiced herring, then strawberries, both cultivated and wild, followed by bilberries and cloudberries, mange-tout peas, yellow chanterelles and ceps, and finally crayfish.

At their cottages, people are happy to go to sauna and sit around a barbeque, and delicious aromas rise from the charcoal or electric grill. The most common things to barbeque are sauna sausage, pork chops or spare ribs. Another popular means of cooking out of doors is a broad, shallow cast-iron pan, the Finns' own wok, which is at its best for making large, wafer-thin pancakes, but which can also be used to fry fish, especially small vendace coated in rye flour.

If you meet someone in the street carrying a bag of peas they have probably come from the market place. Practically everyone develops a passion for fresh peas in summer. Most people eat them raw, but you can also cook them whole in a little water.

The main celebration at this time of year is Midsummer's Eve, when there is practically no

Previous spread:
There are many restaurants on the coast and islands that are open just for the summer months. The photograph is of the NJK restaurant on an island off Helsinki.

Strawberry cake is a delight reserved for the height of summer, which is also the time for the various summer drinks: *sima*, fruit juices and blackcurrant leaf cordial.

A summer menu

- Summer soup
- Smoked fish, new potatoes with dill, herb sauce
- Strawberry and meringue cake
- Coffee

night and the Finnish flag with its blue cross can be flown round the clock. Many people celebrate with bonfires, preferably on a lake shore, provided there is no restriction because of the risk of forest fires. Otherwise it is a time for sauna, swimming and good food.

Although the first early potatoes are available around Whitsun on the south coast, the real season for these begins at Midsummer. New potatoes flavoured with dill are one of the highlights of the summer, and there is always much discussion over what is the right way to cook them. The time when you can lift the first potatoes from your "own patch" and eat them with herring or lightly salted salmon is a moment of true happiness.

Traditional Midsummer foods vary from one part of the country to another. In Häme the usual food eaten at night is little pancakes, while in Ostrobothnia they make a "pink whey" from the liquid remaining from cheese-making, which solidifies after it is cooked for a long time and can be eaten with a spoon.

Potatoes and root vegetables

"Smaller than an egg, and even-sized. Can be cleaned by brushing." That is what new potatoes should be like. Those grown under muslin on the south coast that mark the first fresh vegetables of the season come onto the market around the middle of June, and the best month for new potatoes grown in the open is July, which is when most people lift the first ones in their own fields or gardens and the dill that adds that little extra taste to them is also at its best.

Potatoes have always been the cornerstone of Finnish cooking and a major source of starch, vitamin C and minerals. They can be baked in a dish in the oven, mashed or diced for use in potato salads. Jacket

Summer foods:

Outdoor and barbeque foods: *loimulohi* (glow-fried salmon), *rantakala* (fish stew cooked over an open fire), fried vendace, *rosvopaisti* (a joint of lamb cooked under hot stones or embers from a fire), sauna sausage and *muurinpohjaletut*, savoury or sweet pancakes.

Early potatoes and vegetables, peas, lightly salted fish, the new season's spiced herrings, summer soup, *viili* (a fermented milk product) and cultivated and wild berries and mushrooms.

potatoes baked in the oven are an ancient Finnish custom, while French fries, which were once regarded as festive fare, are now popular as a snack. Potatoes are also used a great deal in baking, as a flour to add to bread or as a pie filling.

Nauris, a small yellow variety of turnip which was a source of vitamin C for the Finns in the days before the potato, is still grown, and is usually ready to pull by the middle of the summer. Children love to eat these raw, while grown-ups also like them baked in the oven or cooked slowly, in a soup or as a pie filling.

Root vegetables grown in Finnish soils are particularly sweet and tasty. Even the smallest of children are familiar with carrots, as they are used for the snowman's nose in winter, but beetroots are also popular, usually pickled in vinegar.

Swede, celery and parsnip are familiar household vegetables that have been rediscovered in recent times and are now highly valued in restaurant circles, so they are once more fully entitled to appear on the table, either to be enjoyed raw or as an ingredient in prepared dishes.

Swede is a sweet vegetable that is excellent grated raw and is also frequently served cooked and either diced or shredded, or baked in the oven along with other root vegetables. It is known best of all, however, in the form in which it appears in Christmas meals or on buffet tables, as *lanttulaatikko*, a fluffy purée baked in the oven.

Summer soup
(kesäkeitto)

1 litre water
1/2 tbsp salt
2 medium-sized carrots
a small cauliflower
1–2 dl fresh green peas
2 dl pods of mange-tout peas
5–6 new potatoes
1–2 tbsp flour
1/2 litres milk
a few fresh spinach leaves
butter
1 tsp sugar
for garnishing:
finely chopped parsley and chives

Heat the water and add salt.
Slice and add the carrots and cook for about 5 minutes.
Dice the cauliflower and potatoes and add them to the soup with the peas and pea pods. When the vegetables are almost done, mix the flour and milk and add to the soup.
Simmer until all the ingredients are done. Add the spinach, and then the sugar and a knob of butter, and sprinkle with parsley and chives.
Serve with dark bread or crispbread.

Smoked food tastes of summer

Smoked food fits in excellently with the Finnish approach to life. It reminds one of so many things: mostly summer, sauna and hygiene. We speak of meat smoked in the sauna when it has been cured at a relatively low temperature. In the olden days this really did happen in the sauna, a smoke sauna with no chimney, which was used for meat and people alternately, but now similar conditions can be reproduced by other means. At one time the temperatures at which salted meat was smoked were very low, and the process could last as long as a week, but nowadays higher temperatures are used. It is also possible to prepare meat by cold smoking, however, where the temperature is still lower and the time required longer. Where warm-smoked meat or fish resembles its oven-cooked counterpart in texture, the product obtained by cold smoking has a shiny gleam about it.

People who smoke meat or fish at home have mostly designed and built boxes or barrels of their own for this, although smoking ovens are also available commercially. The usually woods added for flavour are either alder or juniper, separately or in varying proportions, although a fine flavour can also be obtained with apple wood shavings.

Disposable smoking bags are a relatively new Finnish invention that can be of great help when smoking meat or fish for home use.

The gastronomic traveller may well come across a smoked meats factory on his journey, and wonderful discoveries can sometimes be made at these regardless of whether they are small local firms or large industrialized ones. When fresh local fish such as flounder, perch, bream, Baltic herrings or vendace are thrust straight into the smoking ovens they gain a deliciously golden sheen.

The smoking of fish and meat is an art, and many places have their own experts in this, to whom the hunters, fishermen and livestock breeders bring their produce, such as elk, deer, reindeer, wild boar or pork, to be processed.

Long-awaited summer foods in the coastal areas: smoked flounders, malt bread from the archipelago, peas in their pods, radishes, new potatoes and chives.

Gourmet food from nature:
whitefish tartare, small chantarelles
and a nettle soufflé.

Whitefish (lavaret) tartare

600 g fresh salted whitefish (lavaret)
1 dl mayonnaise
2 finely chopped shallots (50 g)
1 tbsp finely chopped chives
1 tbsp finely chopped dill
1 tsp strong mustard (e.g. Dijon)
2 tbsp lemon juice
black pepper from a mill
(salt)

Quickly fry the shallots in oil and cool them.
Cut the fish into tiny cubes.
Mix the herbs, mustard, cooled shallots and seasoning into the mayonnaise. Finally add the fish cubes to the mayonnaise. Allow to stand in the cold for a couple of hours before serving.
Place a metal ring on the serving plate and fill it with the tartare mixture. Lift off the ring and serve on the same plate with the chantarelle salad and nettle soufflé (see below).

Note:
As a variation, a good salmon tartare can be made in the same way but using rainbow trout or salmon.

Chanterelle salad

1 dl chanterelles, lightly fried in a drop of oil
1 dl diced tomatoes
2 tbsp finely chopped stems of spring onions
for the sauce:
1 tbsp lemon juice
3 tbsp olive oil
salt and a smattering of sugar

Mix the mushrooms, diced tomato and spring onion stems together.
Mix the sauce ingredients together and combine with the others. Check for taste.

Nettle soufflé

(ABOUT 8 INDIVIDUAL PORTIONS)

30 g nettles, boiled and with the water drained off (= 2 litres fresh nettles)
1 potato (50 g)
1/2 dl cream
1 tbsp cornflour
salt and nutmeg
2 egg whites (150 g)

Peel and dice the potato and cook it in the cream.
Grease a set of small portion-sized dishes.
Reduce the nettles to a purée together with the potato and cream. Cool this and add the cornflour and seasoning.
Whip the egg whites to a stiff froth and fold into the potato and nettle mixture.
Serve out into individual ovenproof dishes and cook at 180°C for about 12 minutes. Serve immediately, either in the dishes or with these removed, alongside the whitefish tartare.

Crayfish – gastronomic delights with claws

One important moment for the summer gourmet is midday on 21st July, as it is then that the crayfish season begins – just like an early Christmas for some people. There are many Finns living abroad who try to time their holidays to coincide with the crayfish. The real, original crayfish, *Astacus astacus*, has now been joined by the signal crayfish, *Pacifastacus leniusculus*, introduced into Finland in 1967. The high season is without doubt July and August, which is also when the flowering dill necessary for cooking crayfish is at its best.

If the crayfish on the table really are of the original species, you should make the most of the opportunity, for they are enormously expensive, although a true devotee will not complain but will be prepared to pay for this delicacy. Crayfish are more of a ritual than a food, and should be eaten slowly and meticulously, each person in his own style, as not a scrap should be wasted.

Crayfish parties can be held at home, at a restaurant or at special gatherings. There is an aroma of flowering dill and an atmosphere of celebration in the air. The diners are in a jovial mood and the gastronomic delights are often accompanied by drinking songs. If there are a lot of crayfish, other courses are scarcely necessary, but if there are only a few they can be served as starters to be followed by a main course and dessert.

The crayfish, *Astacus astacus*, is the centrepiece of the meal on August evenings.

Boiled crayfish

40 medium-sized live crayfish
5 litres water
1 1/2 dl coarse sea salt
1–2 sugar cubes
plenty of dill crowns
plenty of dill leaves

Bring the water to the boil and add salt and sugar. Make sure that all the crayfish are alive before you put them in, head first. Keep the water boiling as you add each crayfish. Cover with plenty of dill crowns.

When all the crayfish have been added, cook for 8–10 minutes. Remove from the heat.

Take out the dill and put in new dill. Cool the crayfish in the water as quickly as possible.

Store in a cold place. Serve cold after 4–24 hours, with toast and butter, chopped dill, beer and schnapps or white wine.

A crayfish menu

- Boiled crayfish, toast, dill
- Roast wild duck
- Crème caramel

Going Fishing

Fishing is a popular form of recreation.

Fishing is a popular pastime in Finland, involving all manner of local and national competitions, events and camps in summer and winter. Anyone can go fishing with a hook and line, or through a hole in the ice in winter, but persons aged 18–64 years need a permit for other forms of fishing that represents a payment for fishery management services. Even so, one can't go and fish just anywhere. Especially for angling with a lure or fishing with nets it is essential to have permission from the owner of the fishing rights over the waters concerned and to buy a provincial angling permit.

Sport and recreational fishing, primarily of perch, roach and pike, accounts for a third of total fish catches in this country, while the commercial fishermen, the numbers of whom have dwindled alarmingly, tend to concentrate on more valuable species and on Baltic herring and vendace.

The increased demand for fish has also stimulated fish farming, in the form of both the raising of young fish for stocking purposes and the raising of fish for sale. This latter activity began in the 1960s with the farming of rainbow trout and has now expanded to include whitefish, arctic char and brown trout, and has proved an excellent way of obtaining a regular supply of high quality, definitely unpolluted fish. The latest species to be raised and marketed is sturgeon.

"Fish keeps you beautiful, the harvest from the waters keeps you active," as the saying goes.

We eat a lot of fish in this country of many thousands of lakes, and if you can't manage to go fishing yourself, you can always admire the selection in the markets or on the fish counters of supermarkets. The Finns are encouraged to eat two meals of fish a week, varying the species as much as possible.

Mustard dressing

1/2 dl French mustard
1/2 dl prepared mustard
salt
freshly ground black pepper
2 tbsp sugar
1/2 dl wine vinegar
2 1/2 dl salad oil
2 tbsp finely chopped dill

Mix together the mustards, salt, sugar, black pepper and a drop of the wine vinegar. Beat well. Add the oil as you would in making mayonnaise. Add the remaining wine vinegar a little at a time between the additions of oil. Mix in the finely chopped dill. Parsley and chives can also be used. This dressing is excellent with salted fish or salads containing salted fish. If you want to serve it with meat, reduce the amount of sugar to 25 g. The dressing can also be improved with a few drops of schnapps, brandy or madeira.

Perch, *ahven, Perca fluviatilis*
Looked on as the national fish, the perch is the number one species for recreational fishermen and the delight of those fishing with a hook and line. Even the youngest of fishermen know that this fish with red fins makes a wonderful soup, and being low in fat, it is also tasty fried, grilled or smoked. It is said that, "There's less fat in a perch's head than in a poor man's pantry." Although the legends tell of perch weighing more than three kilos, those caught in a cage or on a hook are normally about ten centimetres long or a bit more. Perch are also good in *kalakukko* or cooked under a crust in a pot, as the bones soften until you don't notice them at all if you cook the fish for long enough.

Pike, *hauki, Esox lucius*
Although this fish is at its best at weights of around 1–2 kilos, fishermen always have their sights set on a big pike. Pike is best minced, in fish loaves or fish balls (quenelles), or else it can be poached and served with a sauce containing hard-boiled egg, or baked in the oven. Pike is the traditional Christmas fish in the archipelago, and the people of Åland have the custom of presenting the President of Finland with a specially chosen large pike as a Christmas greeting, this being the fish for which the province is best known.

Pike-perch, or zander, *kuha, Stizostedion lucioperca*
This fish associated with the province of Uusimaa is to be found in both lakes and the sea. Its fine white flesh and the ease of boning it makes it a favourite in restaurants, where it is usually poached, fried or baked in the oven. An especially delicious accompaniment for pike-perch is grated horse-radish cooked slowly in butter.

Fish stew *(rantakala)* is traditionally cooked on an open fire on the shore.

Fish stew made over an open fire on the shore *(rantakala)*

1 kg cleaned vendace or whitefish (lavaret)
salt
2 onions cut into rings
4–5 potatoes
100–150 g butter
10 whole allspice
water
chives or stems of spring onions

Clean, rinse and drain the vendace. Peel the potatoes and cut them into slices about a centimetre thick.
Place the fish, the slices of potato, spices, onion rings and thin slivers of butter in layers in a cooking pot, with fish forming the top layer.
Add water until the fish at the top are practically covered and cook for about an hour on an open fire.
Chop the chives onto the surface.
Eat with rye bread.

The fish are usually coated in rye flour before they are fried.

Baltic herring fillets *(silakkapihvit)*

1 kg Baltic herrings,
or 500 g Baltic herring fillets,
sprats or fresh sardines
salt, white pepper
dill, chives
for flouring the herrings:
rye flour, salt
for frying:
butter or margarine

Open up the fish with scissors, clean and rinse and remove the head and backbone. Place half of the fillets skin downwards on a board.

Sprinkle with salt and white pepper and a layer of chopped dill and chives. Place an unseasoned fillet on top of each.

Turn the pairs of fillets in a mixture of rye flour and salt. Fry until a golden brown, and serve hot straight from the pan.

If you want to serve the fish with a sauce, add cream to the pan after frying. When it boils, the sauce is ready.

Whitefish, or lavaret, *siika, Corregonus lavaretus*
The whitefish is to be found in lakes and sea areas throughout the country as far as Northern Finland, and is particularly linked to Ostrobothnia. It is an excellent, relatively fast-growing species for farming, and as its flesh is light in colour, fine-grained and very tasty, it is often eaten just lightly salted. There exist innumerable versions of whitefish soup, with or without milk. Smoked whitefish is very commonly found on the fish counters of shops.

Baltic herring, *silakka, Clupea harengus membras*
This little fish with a great taste is a close relative of the herring that is endemic to the Baltic Sea and is recognised as the provincial fish of Southwestern Finland. The fresher it is, the better. When just pulled up out of the water it is a glistening silver colour, stiff as a rod, bluish-green on the back and with a fresh tang about it. The best Baltic herrings are those bought straight from the fishmonger, in the market place or market hall. The cook's life is made easier, of course, if they are bought ready boned and filleted.

They are traditionally fried whole or in double fillets, in both cases dipped in rye flour or finely crushed crispbread crumbs and fried in butter. One other popular way is to grill them over the embers of a wood or charcoal fire, and they are also incomparably good smoked until their skins are a golden brown.

Sprats, *kilohaili, Sprattus sprattus*
Sprats are used mainly for preserving in a sweetish spiced, peppery marinade coloured with sandalwood to produce the Scandinavian equivalent of anchovy. They are smaller than Baltic herrings and can be used for most of the same recipes.

Salmon, *lohi, Salmo salar*

Trout, *taimen, Salmo trutta*

Although imported salmon has become an everyday commodity, both of these fish are likely to remain the marks of festive occasions for the Finns, especially when the host has caught the fish himself. Salmon from the Teno (Tana) River on the Norwegian border is especially highly valued.

The salmon is the provincial fish of Lapland, and lake salmon of Karelia, but there are now restrictions for wild salmon in the Baltic Sea.

Arctic char, *rautu, Salvelinus alpinus*

This rare delicacy that sport fishermen can usually only dream of is another member of the salmon family. Lovers of fish foods, however, can be consoled that the farming of arctic charr in pools has proved fairly successful. The only difference is that the flesh is light in colour where that of specimens caught in the wild is pinkish.

Rainbow trout, *kirjolohi, Oncorhyncus mykiss*

This is a popular everyday food. Supplied by fish farms and easy to bone, fillet and prepare, it is suitable for most culinary purposes. It is also sold lightly salted, cold and warm-smoked and tinned. It can also be prepared by glow-frying over a fire or gas burner, the latter system being a Finnish invention that has been demonstrated abroad on many occasions.

Eel, *ankerias, Anguilla anguilla*

Fresh eels are rare on fish stalls nowadays, and eels are in any case on the decline in nature, although efforts are being made to revive the population by stocking suitable waterways with young eels. They are at their most delicious smoked.

A west-coast speciality – crucified whitefish, cooked in the glow of an open fire.

"Crucified" whitefish or salmon

a whitefish or rainbow trout weighing about 1–2 kg

1 tbsp salt/kg of fish

Clean the fish and split it beside the backbone so that it can be opened easily.

Sprinkle with salt and keep in a cold place for a couple of hours.

Spread the fish out, skin-side down, on a wooden board with a long handle. Nail it to the board with clean wooden pegs or metal nails.

Stand the board by an open fire out of doors, or lean it over the embers of a fire, without the fire actually touching the fish.

The cooking process is slow and should take about an hour.

When the fish is brown and suitably cooked, take it off the board.

Serve with melted butter or with mushroom sauce and boiled potatoes.

Filleting a grayling in the midst of the Lapland countryside.

Vendace, *muikku*, *Corregonus albula*

The best place to try vendace is at a market or demonstration of local foods. Small vendace dipped in rye flour and fried in butter are incomparably delicious – and should be eaten whole, heads, bones and all. They can also be prepared in the same way at home, of course.

The adipose fin shows that the vendace is a member of the salmon family. It is a lake fish, the treasure of Finland's freshwater fishing grounds, and has also been referred to as the aristocrat among the country's fish. Although the people of Eastern Finland regard it as a speciality of theirs, it can be found in abundance in most parts of the country, from south to north. It varies in size, however, from the "needle vendace", which are about five centimetres long, to giant specimens of around twenty centimetres.

This provincial fish of the Savo region has now become the pet species all over the country. It is a safe fish to eat, as it accumulates very little in the way of environmental toxins, but it is also one that should be eaten very fresh. This means that part of the vendace catch ends up being cooked into soup on the shore of

Salmon and potato casserole *(lohilaatikko)*

250–400 g fresh or lightly salted salmon
12–15 medium-sized potatoes (1 kg)
1–2 onions
butter or margarine
2–3 tbsp finely chopped dill
(salt)

for the egg and milk mixture:
2 eggs
4 dl milk
1 tsp salt
a couple of turns of a white pepper mill

for garnishing:
1–2 tbsp dried breadcrumbs
some knobs of butter

Chop the onion and cook in the butter or margarine until transparent. Peel the potatoes and cut both them and the salmon into slices or strips.

the lake in which it was caught, as soon as the catch has been landed. Vendace are usually caught with gill nets, seine nets or trawl nets. The process of pulling in a seine net is a veritable drama for which there is no entry fee.

Tinned vendace, the Finns' own sardines, are usually smoked and then canned in oil or tomato sauce. Vendace roe, which is obtained in autumn, is one of the most highly prized, and expensive, delicacies in Finland.

Lamprey, *nahkiainen*, *Lampetra fluviatilis*

Just speaking of lampreys is enough to whet the appetite of a real gourmet. The lamprey season begins on 18th August and goes on well into the New Year, lasting until the end of March, although the arrival of winter tends to bring the catching of lampreys to an end earlier. At the height of the season warm, freshly fried lampreys are enjoyed especially in Satakunta, where this is the provincial fish.

Lampreys are cyclostomes, snake-like aquatic creatures with a circular, open mouth. They are usually eaten fried or grilled over the embers of a fire, accompanied by mustard sauce and frequently a glass of schnapps. Fried lampreys can be eaten with the fingers, but the real controversy rages over whether you should start from the head or the tail. Grilled lampreys can be bought from fish shops throughout the year, usually in a vinegar marinade flavoured with whole peppers, bay leaves and onion or tinned in oil.

Flounder, *kampela*, *Platicthys flesus*

This is a speciality of the coastal areas and islands that is rare on fish counters elsewhere in the country. People who spend the summer in the archipelago tell

Place the potatoes in a sieve and rinse quickly in running water. Grease an oven dish and arrange half of the slices of potato on the bottom, followed by the salmon and some chopped dill. If you use fresh salmon, season it with salt. Cover the salmon with another layer of potatoes. Whip the eggs, add the milk and season with salt and pepper, then pour this mixture into the dish and sprinkle the surface with breadcrumbs and a few knobs of butter.
Cook in a 175°C oven for
1–1 1/2 hours.
You can also make a Baltic herring casserole in the same way, but place a layer of fatty pork or bacon on top of the fish, add more fish and potatoes and put more fatty pork or bacon on the surface.

of fishermen who smoke these and sell them straight from their boats. Family fishermen also jelly them, but they are at their finest fried or immediately after they have been smoked.

Bream, *lahna, Abramis brama*
The spring-spawning bream is a tasty but bony fish. Those who appreciate the flavour don't care about the bones but simply enjoy its taste and soft texture. Large bream in particular are best smoked, baked in the oven or charcoal grilled. After boiling the fish and extracting the bones it is excellent in aspic jelly. The bream is the provincial fish of Häme.

Burbot, *made, Lota lota*
The burbot is a seasonal fish, the most sought after of those available in winter, when it is normally caught with hooks or nets under the ice. Stewed or made into a soup, it is one of the most longed-for fish dishes of the early winter, and its fine-grained roe is especially valuable and delicious. Some skilful cooks have recently developed new burbot dishes, although it is very good simply fried.

Ruffe, *kiiski, Gymnocephalus cernuus*
Bull-rout, *simppu, Myoxocephalus scorpius*
These are small fish, but are highly prized for making fish stock. They are also caught for their roe, which is orange in colour in the ruffe and turquoise in the bull-rout.

Smelt, *kuore, Osmerus eperlanus*
This almost translucent fish is endemic all along the Finnish coast and in inland lakes, and is often found in catches of Baltic herring. It has a powerful smell, and can occur in shoals during spawning time.

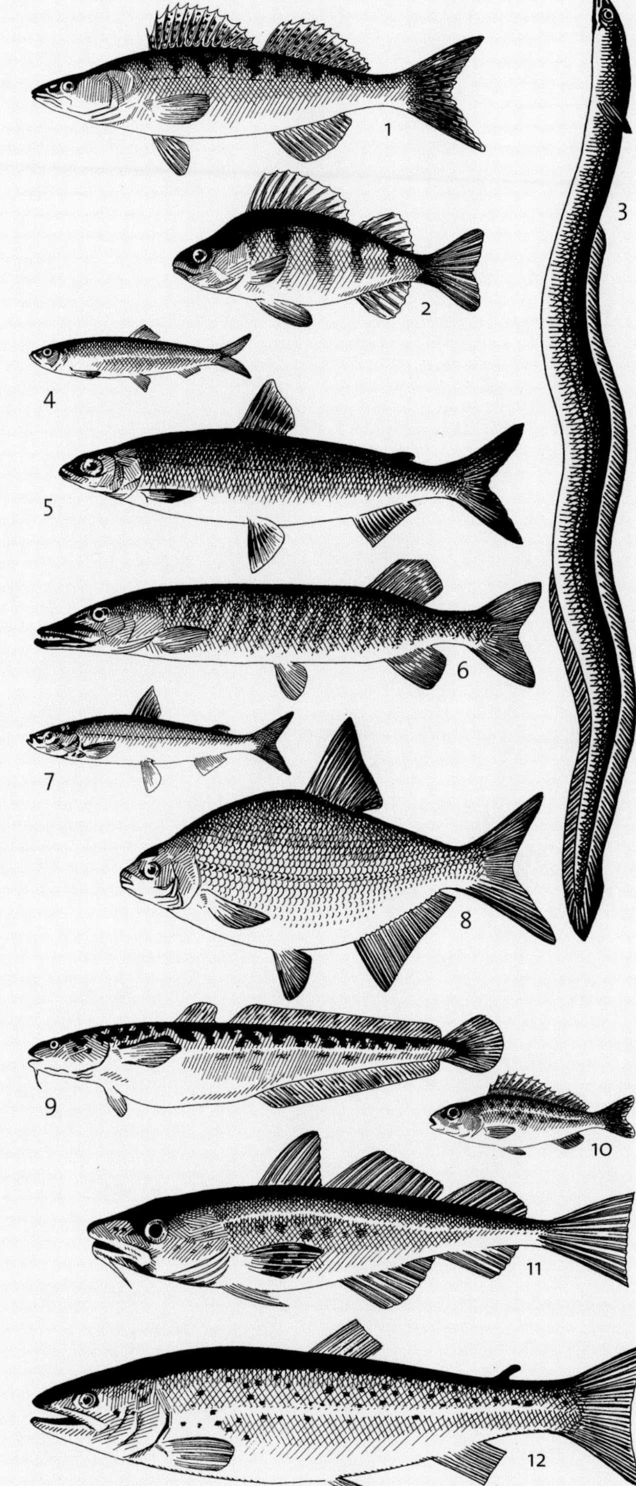

1. Pike-perch / zander, kuha, *Lucioperca lucioperca*
2. Perch, ahven, *Perca fluviatilis*
3. Eel, ankerias, *Anguilla anguilla*
4. Baltic herring, silakka, *Clupea harengus membras*
5. Whitefish (lavaret), siika, *Coregonus lavaretus*
6. Pike, hauki *Esox lucius*
7. Vendace, muikku, *Coregonus albula*
8. Bream, lahna, *Abramis brama*
9. Burbot, made, *Lota lota*
10. Ruffe, kiiski, *Acerina cernua*
11. Cod, turska, *Gadus morhua*
12. Salmon, lohi, *Salmo salar*

Fried pike-perch with crayfish sauce and puréed peas.

Fried pike-perch (zander) with crayfish sauce and mashed peas

150–200 g skinned fillet of pike-perch per person
unsalted butter
salt and white pepper

for the crayfish sauce:
100 g crayfish tails
1 dl melted butter
2 tbsp dill crowns
150 g horseradish
salt and white pepper

for the sauce:
4 shallots, finely diced
3 tbsp butter
3 dl white wine
6 dl crayfish or fish stock
4 dl whipping cream
a pinch of cayenne pepper
salt and white pepper

Lightly fry the shallots for the sauce in butter, but do not brown them. Add the white wine and boil until there is about 1 dl of wine left. Add the crayfish or fish stock and boil until there is 4 dl of liquid left. Finally add the cream and seasoning and reduce for another 15 minutes or so. Sieve.

Finely grate the horseradish and fry it in clarified butter in a pan. There should be enough butter to cover the horseradish and ensure that it turns a golden brown. Be careful, because horseradish burns easily.

Turn the horseradish into a sieve and dab any excess fat off the surface with kitchen paper. Heat the crayfish tails in a small amount of butter just before serving. Add the dill crowns and browned horseradish. Adjust the seasoning with a pinch of salt and pepper.

Fry the fillet of fish lightly on both sides in butter until a golden brown in colour. Season with salt and white pepper.

for the mashed peas:
200 g fresh peas
2 shallots
2 dl mild chicken stock
4 tbsp butter
1/2 dl whipping cream

Finely chop the onions and fry them lightly.
Add the stock and peas and cook until done.
Finally add the butter and cream. Season and cook for another 2 minutes.

Reduce to a purée. Check for taste and add salt if necessary. If you want the mashed peas to be completely smooth, press the mixture through a sieve as well.

Blinis at their finest: with fish roe, smetana and chopped onions.

Fish roe

When one passenger asked the air hostess, "Caviar, what is it?", she replied "It's fish eggs," to which the response came, "Then can I have two, please?"

Fish spawn at different seasons of the year, some in spring, others in autumn or in winter. The most sought-after are burbot, vendace and whitefish roe, although true gourmets know equally well when to ask for ruffe or smelt roe.

There is a certain ritual that belongs to eating roe. Each ingredient, the roe and the things that accompany it, such as chopped onion, whipped cream or smetana, should be put out in a separate dish, together with mills containing various kinds of pepper. The diners can then combine these just as they wish, season the mixture with pepper and spread it on either dark or white toast, blinis or jacket potatoes, or eat it with boiled potatoes. Roe can also be used in sauces or as a garnish for fish.

The Baltic herring spawns in April or May, and its roe is pale yellow in colour, the eggs small in size and the texture rather hard, so that it grates on the teeth. The taste is fairly neutral. Ruffe and smelt roe is a beautiful shade of yellow, but both species are rarely found in the shops, although in many people's opinion they are still finer to the taste than vendace roe, which resembles them somewhat. Vendace and whitefish roe are both autumn products, the former being fine in texture and a deep orange-yellow in colour, while the latter is coarser and paler. The finest-grained of all, and the mildest in taste, is burbot roe, the flavour of which is rendered still milder by the fact that it is often mixed with whipped cream. It can also be served together with small cubes of onion and cooked burbot liver, or else the cooked liver can be mashed and mixed into the roe.

Blinis

2 dl lukewarm milk
25 g fresh yeast, or 11 g dried yeast
1 dl cream
2 dl plain flour
3 dl buckwheat flour
about 4 dl hot milk
about 1 tsp salt
2 tbsp melted butter
2 eggs

Crumble the fresh yeast into the water or sprinkle the dried yeast on top of the water to dissolve it.
Add the cream and whip in the plain flour and buckwheat flour.
Let the batter stand, preferably for 2 hours or overnight.
Add the hot milk, salt, melted butter and egg yolks to the batter.
Whip the whites and fold them in just before frying.
Fry on both sides in a special blini pan or pancake pan.
Serve hot straight from the pan.

Many people also choose ground allspice to season burbot roe.

Time will tell whether Finland is destined to become a producer of black caviar, but we had the first taste of such a caviar in 2005, from three female sturgeon raised in the cooling water of one of the Stora Enso pulp mills.

Kalakukko

The Finnish *kalakukko* is the cleverest and most unusual container in which to preserve fish, as the outside casing can be eaten, too. It has now been registered with the European Union as an Authentic Traditional Product, so that the name and method of producing it are protected. It can be produced anywhere at all, but the product can only be called *kalakukko* if the traditional method is followed.

The people of Eastern Finland have been eating *kalakukko* since the Middle Ages, as apart from being especially tasty, it was easy to take with you on a journey, to the market or to church, for instance. There are differences from one area to another in how it is made, cut and eaten, however. The ancestor of the *kalakukko* is the Karelian *kurniekka*, a fish baked inside a loaf of bread, and the pastry crust can be either leavened rye bread or merely rye flour mixed with water and a little salt. The people of Savo open the round *kalakukko* by cutting a hole in the top with a sheath knife, while in Northern Karelia they cut it into slices. In Kuopio, the city of the *kalakukko*, they have developed an elongated version that is cut across and pieces are sold under the English name of Kukko Slice.

A *kalakukko* can be filled with vendace, perch, rainbow trout or burbot, or alternatively it is

Fish pie in a rye bread crust *(kalakukko)*

for the crust:
5 dl water
1/2 tbsp salt
100 g soft butter or margarine
about 9 dl rye flour
about 3 dl plain or bread flour
for the filling:
1 kg whole vendace or
small perch, or pieces of
rainbow trout or burbot
150–250 g strips of fatty pork
2–3 tbsp salt

Mix the ingredients for the crust together and knead into a stiff, tight dough. Pat it down or roll it out on a well-flouered board to form an oval slab about 1 1/2 cm thick in the centre and thinner at the edges. Sprinkle the centre part with rye flour. Clean the fish and strain well, then arrange them in alternate layers with the pork fat in the centre of the dough. Sprinkle a little salt on top of each layer. The top layer should be pork fat.

Turn the sides of the dough up around and on top of the filling to form the pie crust and smooth it over with water and flour. (Keep a small piece of dough on one side for plugging the crust, then wrap the pie in aluminium foil and bake for another 4–5 hours at 120–150°C to cook the fish. remove from the oven and cover well in order to soften the crust.

Fish pie in a pot *(patakukko)*

1 kg small perch or vendace, cleaned
250 g sliced belly pork
1 tbsp salt
a drop of water
for the pie dough:
5 dl rye flour
2 dl water
1 tsp salt

Clean the fish and sprinkle with salt. Let them stand for a couple of hours or overnight to salt properly. Place alternate layers of fish and pork in a greased baking dish and add a drop of water.

Make a compact dough of the rye flour, salt and water and cover the dish with it. Bake in a 150–175°C oven for 2–3 hours.

possible to use meat, swede or potato. The important thing is that the fish and vegetables should cook slowly inside the pastry case until they become deliciously soft. They are kept moist during this process by the strips of fatty pork added to them, which make the fish, especially vendace, taste just like sardines.

It is also possible to make open vendace pies, and in Pori on the west coast they bake a form of bread with Baltic herrings interleaved with layers of dough.

Kalakukko, a fish pie with a rye bread crust, is now protected by the EU as a traditional dish. The rye bread crust hides the soft, well-cooked fish and pork inside it.

Autumn Leaves – Mushrooms and Berries

Eventually summer gives way to the wonderful colours of autumn. The deciduous trees and bushes in the south of the country glow with innumerable shades of red and yellow, while in Lapland the splendid colours of the dwarf shrubs on the ground invade the slopes of the fells, the undergrowth in the forests and the vegetation of the bogs. You can expect the first falls of snow in September in Lapland, but usually in October or November in other parts of the country. By this time the summer holidays are over, the schoolchildren have gone back to their desks, country cottages and gardens have been made ready for the winter and it is time to take the boats out of the water.

From a gastronomic point of view, however, the horn of plenty still has much to offer: fish, mushrooms, berries and game from nature and fruit and vegetables from the garden. Various herring and fish markets, *silakkamarkkinat*, provide festive moments for the people living on the coast and islands and provide an opportunity for the fishing families to sell their wares in the coastal towns, mainly spiced fish preserves, especially of Baltic herring, made during the summer. Other items on sale at these markets may include game products, the sweet island bread, home-made juices and jellies made from rowanberries, sea buckthorn berries and cranberries, and handicrafts, sheepskins and various hand-made wooden objects.

On the west coast this is a time for enjoying lampreys, served either in mustard sauce or in a vinegar-based marinade and usually washed down with a small glass of schnapps.

Previous spread:
The word *ruska* stands for the glowing autumn colours that light up the landscape.

Looking for mushrooms is an education even for the smallest members of the family.

An autumn menu

- Vendace, whitefish or rainbow trout roe
- Small cabbage rolls, boiled potatoes and lingonberry jam
- Apple crumble

One of the best things about autumn is the excursions to pick berries and mushrooms. This is when the lingonberries ripen in the forests and the distinctive-flavoured cranberries on the bogs, while the mushroom picker can fill a basket with milk-caps, hedgehog mushrooms, funnel chanterelles and other tasty species. You can sometimes still find chanterelles and boletes even in autumn.

The best part of a trip to pick mushrooms is nevertheless the time when you can sit round the table together afterwards, cleaning and identifying them. As they have to be used fresh, it's good to clean and blanch them at once, ready for cooking or preserving.

Another useful hint is that you should try to wear a red hat if at all possible when you go out into the forest at this time of year, as there may be hunters on the move in search of elk and deer.

Autumn is also the time for gathering in the remainder of the "underground harvest" of potatoes and root vegetables.

Autumn delicacies:

Apples and apple juice, whitefish and vendace roe, lampreys with mustard sauce, mushroom and cabbage dishes, and game in its various forms, such as minced elk meat balls, elk stew or joints of roast elk.

A spiced vinegar marinade puts a new face on fried vendace and Baltic herrings.

Baltic herrings or vendace in vinegar

(Sprats or smelt can also be used.)

1 kg smallish vendace or Baltic herrings
rye flour, salt
for frying:
butter
for the marinade:
1 dl white wine vinegar
1 1/2–2 dl water
2–3 tbsp sugar
a pinch of salt
8 whole allspice
1–2 bay leaves
1 red onion or ordinary onion, sliced into thin rings

Roll the fish in the salted rye flour and fry them on both sides until crisp. Cool.

Mix the ingredients for the marinade, put the fish in a pot or dish and pour the marinade over them so that they are definitely all covered. Keep in the cold for 1/2–1 day before serving.

Cabbage rolls
(kaalikääryleet)

(FOR ABOUT 35 ROLLS)

a large white cabbage (about 2 kg)
water, salt
for the filling:
400 g minced meat, pork and beef
1 1/2 tsp salt
1–2 tsp dried marjoram
1 dl uncooked pudding rice
water, salt
1 small onion
1/2 dl breadcrumbs
1 dl water
1 dl cream
salt, black pepper
for frying:
butter or margarine
for brushing on top:
1 dl treacle
for basting:
1 dl cream

Cut out the stem of the cabbage with a small, sharp knife. Cook the cabbage in salted water until done. Remove and drain the leaves. Pare down the thick base of each leaf.

Cook the rice in salted water, let the breadcrumbs swell in the water and cream mixture, and then mix the minced meat, breadcrumbs, chopped onion, seasoning and rice. Season.

Spread the cabbage leaves out on a board. Put 1–2 tbsp of filling on each leaf, and wrap into little packets. Place these side by side in a greased baking dish. Top with a few knobs of butter and pour treacle on them.

Bake at 225°C until slightly brown. Turn them over and bake them further. Add a little water or stock and cream. Lower the temperature to 180°C, baste and bake for 45–60 minutes.

Serve with lingonberry or cranberry jam or fresh puréed berries.

Cabbage and lamb, baked in the oven
(lammaskaali)

1 kg shoulder or flank of lamb, etc. on the bone
1 1/2–2 kg cabbage
3 carrots
10 whole allspice
2 tsp salt
for frying:
butter, margarine or oil

Chop the cabbage, discarding the hard parts, and peel and slice the carrots.

Cut up the lamb and brown the pieces in hot fat in a frying pan. Place the cabbage, meat, carrots and spices in layers in an ovenproof casserole. Add a little water to the frying pan and pour the juice into the casserole.

Cover and cook in a 200°C oven for 2–2 1/2 hours. Lift the meat out, remove the bones and put the meat back into the casserole.

Serve with tomatoes or lingonberry purée.

"Crayfish" herrings
(rapusilakat)

600 g Baltic herring fillets
(sprats can also be used)
salt, black pepper
a bunch of dill with stalks
2 1/2 dl tomato juice, or the same quantity of
crushed canned tomatoes
butter

Grease a flame-proof casserole, saucepan, or frying pan. Place the fillets, skin-side up, on a chopping board and sprinkle them with salt, black pepper and chopped dill leaves.

Roll the fillets and place them side by side in the casserole or pan. Sprinkle with chopped dill stalks and salt, and cover with tomato juice or crushed tomatoes. Cover and simmer gently for about 15 minutes. Serve cold.

Hamburger à la Lindström
(Lindströmin pihvit)

400 g minced beef
1–1 1/2 tsp salt
1/4 tsp white pepper
1 egg
1 1/2 dl water or cream
1 onion, chopped
1 medium-sized boiled potato, mashed
2 medium-sized pickled beetroots, chopped
(1–2 tbsp capers, chopped)
for frying:
2 tbsp butter or margarine

Lightly fry the chopped onion if you wish. Mix all the ingredients together. Form the mixture into 8–10 hamburgers. Fry for 2–3 minutes on each side. Serve with fried onion rings.

Vegetables baked in the oven

3 carrots
2 parsnips
4 medium-sized potatoes
8 small onions
1 red pepper
2 tsp salt
2 tsp rosemary
1 tsp thyme
about 1/2 dl rapeseed oil

Peel the carrots, parsnips, potatoes and onions. Cut the carrots and parsnips in two lengthways and cut the potatoes and onions in half. Cut the red pepper in half, remove the stalk and seeds, and slice the remainder into eight pieces.

Oil a large oven dish, spread the vegetables out on it and sprinkle with the salt and herbs.

Finally pour the cooking oil on the top. Stir well. Cook in a 175°C oven for about 40 minutes, stirring occasionally.

Apple crumble

4–5 apples
cinnamon
for the crumble:
4 dl rolled porridge oats (quick-cooking)
1 dl sugar
75 g butter or margarine
ground cinnamon

Peel, core, and slice the apples. Grease an ovenproof dish and cover the bottom with slices of apple. Sprinkle with cinnamon.

Combine the oats and sugar. Melt the butter or margarine and add it to the mixture. Spread this mixture over the apples.

Bake at 200°C for about 25 minutes.

Clear wildfowl bouillon, a warm cep salad and crisp flakes of bread.

Clear wildfowl bouillon and warm cep salad

1 1/2 kg wildfowl bones
(willow grouse, pheasant, wild duck, etc.)
2 litres cold water
2 onions, cut into pieces
2 carrots, cut into pieces
a piece of celeriac
1 leek, cut into pieces
1 whole small bulb of garlic
1 sprig of thyme
1 sprig of rosemary
a few whole white and black peppers
1 tbsp sea salt
to flavour the bouillon:
1/2 dl Madeira
1 tbsp cognac

Heat the bones in a 200°C oven for about 1/2 hour, turning them from time to time. Take them out of the oven and pour off the fat. Put the bones in a large saucepan and add the water and other ingredients. Heat to the verge of boiling and scoop the foam off the top with a skimming ladle. Allow the bouillon to boil for 10 minutes, and then reduce the heat and allow it to boil gently for about 3 hours. Sieve the bouillon through a muslin cloth into a clean saucepan, and continue cooking until there is about 8 dl of it left. Check for taste and add the Madeira and cognac just before serving.

Note:

A similar stock can be made totally or in part from chicken bones.

Warm cep salad

100 g cep mushrooms
2 tbsp butter
salt and black pepper
some sprigs of thyme
a few leaves of chervil
a little walnut oil

Clean the ceps and cut them into slices. Fry them in butter until they are golden brown and season with salt. Take them out onto a sheet of kitchen paper to drain. Re-heat them in a frying pan or saucepan before serving with the bouillon.

At that stage put the slices of mushroom in a saucepan and add a drop of oil. Mix the ingredients lightly and quickly while heating them. Season with black pepper, thyme and chervil.

Malt bread crisps

Cut wafer-thin slices off a loaf of malt bread and place them side by side on an oven dish. Dry them in a 120°C oven for 1/2–1 hour until crisp

Gathering Mushrooms

The "silent hunting season" begins each year at the time when the wild mushrooms appear in their accustomed places in the forests. Harvests vary greatly from one year to the next, and also between species, so that we can speak of false morel, bolete, milk-cap or chanterelle years separately. Experienced, sharp-eyed pickers can spot mushrooms all over the place: yellow chanterelles in birch groves, boletes on the edges of ditches or fields and in spruce forests, and funnel chanterelles on moss-covered rocky slopes. Different mushrooms can be found in the yards of houses, beside roads, in fields, on bogs and above all in forests, and if you fail to find any at all, at least the exercise of looking for them is good for you.

Those who pick mushrooms for home use will usually take the first ones for eating straight away and then start preserving some for the winter. There are hundreds of species of mushrooms in the forests, of which about twenty are approved as commercial species. During the season there are often advisors at the market place in towns to help people identify the mushrooms they have picked.

A conscious effort is being made to promote the use of mushrooms, with the aim of finding more people to take this up commercially. Many places have collecting points where pickers can sell their mushrooms to a dealer, the most popular species for this being the boletes. This can be an appreciable source of extra non-taxable income in a good year for ceps.

A good selection of autumn mushrooms: funnel chantarelles, yellow chantarelles and woolly milk-caps.

Use is made of preserved mushrooms, either salted, dried or frozen, all the year round and in many different ways. As well as chopping them into small pieces and frying them, marinading them or making them into a soup or salad, some homes put milk-caps into *rieska* or make mushroom bread or cep pancakes. Mushroom pies are also popular with visitors, and various wild mushrooms can be sprinkled on pizza.

Cultivated champignons, oyster mushrooms and shiitake mushrooms are available throughout the country. Recent innovations include a pickle-like mushroom preserve and a cheese spread flavoured with horn-of-plenty mushrooms.

The false morel, *Gyromitra esculenta*, *korvasieni*, is a highly-prized spring mushroom with a variety of uses, but is poisonous unless properly treated. It can be preserved by drying and freezing. It should be boiled twice for five minutes each in plenty of water (three parts of water to one part of mushrooms), throwing the water away each time and rinsing and draining the mushrooms thoroughly. Dried false morels should be soaked first and then treated in the same way as fresh ones. The water in which these mushrooms have been soaked or boiled should on no account be used.

The cep, or penny bun mushroom, *Boletus edulis*, can be cleaned and put directly into the frying pan, or else it can be dried and frozen. It is good in soups, stews, finely chopped and fried or in pies.

The yellow chanterelle, *Cantharellus cibarius*, can similarly be cleaned and used directly. This, too, can be finely chopped and fried or else used in a soup or stew, and can also be pickled. It keeps best frozen.

The horn-of-plenty, *Craterellus cornucopioides*, can be used directly in soups or pies and can be finely chopped and fried. It is easy to preserve by drying.

The funnel chanterelle, *Cantharellus tubaeformis*, is a late autumn mushroom that can be cooked directly. It can also be frozen or dried.

The ordinary milk-cap, *Lactarius trivialis*, must first be boiled in water. It can then be used in

Mushroom and cheese quiche

for the base:

150 g butter or margarine
3 dl plain flour
2 tbsp cold water

for the filling:

1 litre fresh funnel chanterelles, ceps, champignons or shiitake
1 leek
rapeseed oil
salt, black pepper
1 tsp thyme or tarragon

for the egg and milk mixture:

2 eggs
1 dl milk
1 dl thick cream
1 tsp salt

for garnishing:

2 dl grated cheese

Work the butter or margarine into the flour with your fingers. When the mixture has a granular texture, add the water and mix to a dough by hand. Allow the dough to stand in the fridge for about an hour, then form it into a layer to cover the bottom and sides of a quiche dish.

Clean the mushrooms if necessary and chop them into pieces. Finely chop the leek. Heat a frying pan and fry the leek and mushrooms in oil for 10–15 minutes. Season with the salt, pepper and herbs. Cool.

Turn the oven on, with the thermostat at 225°C.
Whip the eggs, milk and cream together and add the salt.
Put the mushroom mixture into the quiche dish and pour the egg and milk on top of it. Sprinkle the surface with grated cheese.
Bake on the lower shelf of the oven for half an hour or more.
The quiche will be done when it is a beautiful brown on the surface and the filling has set.

Variations:

You can give the quiche a smoky flavour by adding 150 g shredded crispy bacon, smoked reindeer meat or smoked ham to the mushrooms.

mushroom salads and sauces. It is usually preserved by salting.

Salted mushrooms should be soaked in cold water for a few hours or overnight before use.

All the milk-cap mushrooms *(Lactarius)* apart from the saffron milk-cap, *Lactarius deliciosus*, need to be boiled in water before use. They may then be frozen, but more often they are preserved by salting. Salted mushrooms must be soaked before use in a large volume of cold water for a few hours or up to 12 hours, depending on the amount of salt in them. The most popular species in Finland is *Lactarius trivialis*. The milk-caps are usually used in sauces, salads, soups and pies, and can also be added to a bread dough.

The wild mushrooms are our "vegetarian game"

Cep, herkkutatti,
Boletus edulis.

False morel, korvasieni,
Gyromitra esculenta.
Poisonous!
Boil several times before use!
See page 88.

Hedgehog fungus, vaaleaorakas,
Hydnum repandum

Saffron milk-cap, männynleppärousku,
Lactarius deliciosus

Milk-cap, haaparousku,
Lactarius trivialis.
Boil before use.

Horn of plenty, mustatorvisieni,
Craterellus cornucopioides

A sweet chantarelle pickle will add spice to meat and game dishes..

Creamed mushrooms *(sienimuhennos)*

1 litre good mushrooms
(chantarelles, ceps, cultivated mushrooms)
1 onion
50 g butter or margarine
2 tbsp plain flour
about 1/2 l milk, or milk and cream
salt, white and black pepper
(a little basil)

Clean the mushrooms and boil them if necessary. Dice those mushrooms that can be used fresh. Drain the boiled mushrooms and chop finely. Dice the onion.

Melt about half of the butter or margarine and add the mushrooms. Cook until the liquid has evaporated. Add the rest of the butter or margarine and the onion, Fry until the onion is transparent.

Sprinkle the flour on the top and add the liquid little by little, stirring constantly.

Simmer under a cover for 10–20 minutes. Add more liquid if necessary. Season to taste with salt and pepper, and with basil if you like.

Mushroom soup

To make a mushroom soup, increase the amount of liquid and replace part of it with stock.

Pickled chantarelles

400 g cleaned small
yellow chanterelles
for the pickling liquid:
2 dl water
1 1/2 dl red wine vinegar
1 tbsp sea salt (20 g)
100 g sugar
1 tsp whole black peppers
1/2 vanilla pod
1/2 dl whole cloves
1/2 dl whole allspice
a piece of dried ginger
1 red onion, chopped
a sprig of rosemary

Measure the water into a saucepan and add the sugar and all the spices. Cook gently for about 15 minutes, then take the saucepan off the heat and add the vinegar.

Put the mushrooms in a clean jar that has a tight lid and pour the hot liquid onto them. Allow to stand for at last 10 hours before serving.

Wild cranberries (*Vaccinium oxycoccus*) are full of healthy antioxidants.

Berry parfait

2 egg yolks
about 1 1/2 dl icing sugar
about 1 1/2 dl cranberry, rowanberry or raspberry purée
4 dl whipping cream

Whisk the egg yolks and sugar to a froth in a bain marie and add the berry purée. Allow to cool.
Whip the cream and fold into the mixture.
Check for taste, and add more sugar if needed. Turn the mixture into a parfait mould or bowl rinsed with cold water and freeze.
To serve, dip the mould in hot water for a few seconds and turn the parfait onto a serving plate. Decorate with whipped cream and more of the berries.
You can make a parfait of this kind from any of the Finnish berries, e.g. rowanberries or raspberries, but the quantities of purée and sugar should be adjusted according to how sharp the berries are.

The Promised Land for Wild Berries

Wild berries develop a powerful aroma in the short summers of these northern latitudes, and have an excellent nutritive value with high proportions of healthy substances. Almost all these berries can be bought frozen in the shops.

It is estimated that the Finns eat about eight kilos of wild berries per person every year, which is about a third of their total intake of fruit and fruit products. Berries are also used to produce delicious jams and liqueurs, in which the secret of their excellent flavour lies in the use of fresh berries instead of essences. It has even been known for berry flavours to be added to beer.

Around Midsummer is usually the time when people go to check on their favourite places for picking the various berries The first task is to see whether the wild strawberries, *Fragaria vesca*, are ripe yet, whether it is time to string them on a blade of grass as we used to do in our childhood, that time long ago when the sun was always shining and it never rained!

The bilberries, or blueberries, *Vaccinium myrtillus*, ripen a little later, in July. This could well be looked on as the national berry, or at least the people's health berry. It grows throughout the length of the country, but the numbers of places where it grows are decreasing alarmingly. Bush varieties for growing in the garden have been developed and have become popular, but the wild berries have a stronger taste.

Fresh bilberries are delicious when eaten with milk on them or in bilberry pie, and bilberry soup, which is available in cartons from shops, is a traditional summer dessert and source of healthy nutrients. It is also much appreciated by athletes, so that the purple stain on a marathon runner's shirt will probably be the result of tanking up with bilberry soup en route It is also given to children as a medicine, and a good helping on one's breakfast porridge provides a comfortable lining for the stomach for the whole day. Recent research has confirmed the role of bilberries as a significant source of phenolic compounds, and has stimulated exports for use in functional foods.

Bilberries can also be mixed with raspberries, *Rubus idaeus*, to produce what is known as the "queen of jams", by far the best topping for the pancakes that the Finns love so much. Wild raspberries are tasty and sweet-smelling and can be successfully frozen.

The most valuable and sought-after of the wild berries is the golden yellow cloudberry, *Rubus chamaemorus*, which grows best on the bogs of Northern Finland and Ostrobothnia. This is rich in vitamin C and has a very concentrated taste, which for the connoisseur is not dimmed by its large number of rather hard seeds. Cloudberries are at their best eaten at room temperature, but they are also used in jams, desserts, ice creams and especially liqueurs.

The arctic bramble, *Rubus arcticus*, resembles a raspberry but is sublime in both taste and aroma. Even the Finns go wild at the prospect of fresh arctic brambles, especially as these are becoming a rarity as the result of intensified forest management. Harvests of wild berries have diminished greatly, but experiments with cultivating them have been promising. A cross between an arctic bramble and a raspberry has also been obtained which is easier to grow in a garden and easer to pick.

The real "red gold" of the Finnish forests and all-time favourite for preserving is the lingonberry, or cowberry, *Vaccinium vitis-idaea*. This again has many healthy properties, containing vitamins A, C and E, folic acid, potassium and calcium and one ingredient of red wine that has been found to be particularly healthy, which is present in almost the same quantities as in grapes. Lingonberries mostly grow in dryish heath forests and ripen in the late summer or early autumn. They can be added to porridges or salads, they can be made into juice, jam and a jelly for eating with meat or blood dishes, and are sometimes added to bread, cake and biscuit doughs. They keep very well when crushed.

The cranberry, *Vaccinium oxycoccus*, is the last of our wild berries to ripen, and can be found among the *Sphagnum* mosses on the surfaces of the bogs. Its flavour will not suffer even if it is caught by the frost a few times; on the contrary, this will improve it. The ruby-red wild cranberries are very much smaller than cultivated ones and are virtually translucent when ripe, with a refined taste. They are used mainly for making juices, jam, jellies and liqueurs, and these again are healthy as well as delicious. They have a low energy content but are rich in fibre, and they contain more antioxidants and phenols than the other berries. They keep well just as they are in a cool cellar, cold store, freezer or open balcony during the winter.

Two species of berry that are unique to these northern parts are the crowberry, *Empetrum nigrum*, and the sea buckthorn, *Hippophaë rhamnoides*. A good harvest of crowberries is usually obtained on the fells of Lapland, and they can be used in juices, jellies, liqueurs and desserts. Their nutritional and aromatic qualities are poorer than those of the sea buckthorn, however.

Wild strawberry, ahomansikka, *Fragaria vesca.*

Arctic bramble, mesimarja, *Rubus arcticus.*

Cloudberry, lakka, *Rubus chamaemorus.*

Raspberry, vadelma, *Rubus idaeus.*

Sea buckthorn, tyrnimarja, *Hippophaë rhamnoides.*

Lingonberry / cowberry, puolukka, *Vaccinium vitis-idaea.*

This latter berry is indigenous to the Åland Islands and the Gulf of Bothnia coast, but new strains have been developed that can be cultivated elsewhere. The spiny branches of this bush carry orange berries that are acid to the taste but extremely rich in vitamin C and also contain large amounts of vitamin A precursors such as beta-carotene and of vitamins E and K. They have also been found to contain plant sterols, which reduce the absorption of cholesterol from food into the body. A juice can be extracted from sea buckthorn berries, and this can also be made into a liqueur.

All these treasures of our forests have been utilized by chefs, restaurateurs and patisseurs, who have developed a whole range of magnificent cakes, pastries and desserts from them. One of the most interesting, however, is the rowanberry, *Sorbus aucuparia*, which has traditionally been used for making jams, jellies and a liqueur. A purée of these berries adds a very good flavour to desserts and sauces, having a pleasantly bitter taste that goes well with game, especially wildfowl.

The Finnish wild berries are much sought-after as raw materials for both the food-processing and pharmaceuticals industries. Dried lingonberries or bilberries can be bought as sweets, even covered in chocolate, and there is an old Russian recipe for cranberries rolled in egg white and dusted with sugar.

Bilberries, or blueberries (*Vaccinium myrtillus*), have always been an important source of nutrition.

Berry salad

Mix together various kinds of berries, preferably wild berries, or group them elegantly in a serving dish. Spatter with a little Arctic bramble or cranberry liqueur.

Serve with whipped cream or ice cream.

Fruit or berry kissel *(mehukiisseli)*

1 litre strong diluted berry or fruit juice
4 tbsp potato flour
sugar to taste

Add sugar to the juice and mix in the potato flour. Bring to the boil, stirring all the time, and then take the saucepan off the heat immediately.

Pour into a serving dish and sprinkle with sugar. Cool.

Serve with milk, cream, or whipped cream.

Whipped berry porridge *(vispipuuro)*

1 litre strong, diluted lingonberry juice
1 1/2 dl semolina
1 1/2 dl sugar
1/4 tsp salt

Heat the juice to boiling point. Whisk in the semolina and cook for about 20 minutes, stirring from time to time.

Let the porridge cool for a while in a cold waterbath, then whip to make a light, fluffy pink dessert.

Serve cold with milk.

Rowanberry jelly

1 kg rowanberries
7 dl water
750 g sugar for 1 litre of juice

Rinse the berries, which should be only partly ripe. Bring the water to the boil and add the berries. Cook with the saucepan lid on for 10 minutes and crush. Sieve and measure the amount of juice obtained. Add the necessary amount of sugar. Cook for a further 20 minutes or so without the lid. Test for setting by putting a drop of the liquid on a cold plate. If it sets, take the jelly off the stove and pour it into clean jars.

Frozen rowanberry purée

1 litre rowanberries
1 dl sugar
water

Cook the rowanberries in a small amount of water until they can be mashed or blended.

Add the sugar.

Use immediately, or place in small containers and freeze.

Strawberry and meringue cake

(FOR 8 PERSONS)

6 egg whites

2 dl sugar

3 dl ground almonds

for sprinkling on the surface:

flaked almonds

Lightly whip the egg whites and add half of the sugar. Then whip them to a stiff froth and add the remaining sugar. Sieve in the ground almonds, and then spread this meringue mixture evenly on a piece of greaseproof paper on an oven tray. Sprinkle flaked almonds on top.

Bake at once in a 150°C oven for about half an hour or longer, until the slab of meringue feels crisp. Cool.

for the vanilla cream:

6 dl milk

6 egg yolks

1 1/2 dl sugar

2 tbsp cornflour

a split vanilla pod

2 dl firm whipped cream

Mix the milk, egg yolks, sugar, cornflour and vanilla pod together. Bring the mixture to the boil, stirring well all the time. Sieve the mixture when it has partially set to the consistency of kissel, and cool. Remove the vanilla pod and add the whipped cream.

for the filling and topping:

1 litre fresh strawberries

Cut the sheet of meringue in two. Place one piece on the serving plate and spread it with slices of strawberry and a layer of vanilla cream. Put the second piece of meringue on top. Decorate and serve immediately.

Bilberry pie *(mustikkapiirakka)*

for the pastry:

150 g butter or margarine

(1/2 dl sugar)

1 egg

1/2 dl cream

2 1/2 dl flour

for the filling:

about 1 litre bilberries

sugar

1–1 1/2 tbsp dried breadcrumbs or potato flour

Beat the butter or margarine to a froth and add sugar if desired. Add the egg, mixing well, then the cream and flour alternately. Don't beat it too much or the dough will become tough.

Let the dough stand in a cool place for a while. With floured hands, spread the dough out on the bottom and sides of a 25–30 cm pie dish and pat it into position.

Mix the bilberries with sugar and dried breadcrumbs or potato flour. Spread this filling onto the dough and raise the edges.

Bake at 200°C for about 30 minutes, until the edges are a golden brown.

It is very much a matter of taste whether bilberry pie should be made with a pastry crust or a *pulla* dough.

Bilberry soup
(mustikkakeitto)

1 litre water

1/2 litre bilberries

1 1/2 dl sugar

2 tbsp potato flour

Put the water, bilberries and sugar in a saucepan. Mix and cook for about five minutes.

Dissolve the potato flour in about 1/2 dl of cold water. Remove the boiling bilberry mixture from the stove and add the potato flour to it, stirring well.

Put the saucepan back on the stove and bring to the boil. Remove from the heat as soon as the first bubbles appear.

Sprinkle with sugar and cool. Serve cold with sweet rusks or biscuits.

Crème caramel

(FOR 4–6 INDIVIDUAL PORTIONS)

4 eggs

2 dl milk

2 dl cream

1 dl sugar

1 vanilla pod

for the syrup:

1 dl sugar

1/2 dl water

Melt the sugar in a saucepan and allow it to burn until it is a golden brown in colour. Add the water. (Be careful, as water can spit when it comes into contact with hot sugar.)

Mix the sugar and water together and cook until they form a syrup of even consistency. Pour this syrup into individual portion-sized ovenproof dishes to form 1 1/2 cm layers on the bottom and allow to cool.

Split the vanilla pod and put it into a saucepan together with the cream, milk and sugar and allow to boil for a moment. Cool.

Whip the eggs until the yolks are broken (but not to a froth!) and mix into the milk and cream. Sieve and pour into the dishes, on top of the syrup.

Cook in a 100°C oven for about 45 minutes, until the mixture sets. Cool.

Turn the puddings out onto plates and surround with berries and juice.

Garnish with cornflower petals, for instance.

for the berries in juice:

raspberries, blackcurrants, cloudberries, gooseberries

for a lime-flavoured juice:

2 dl sugar

1 1/2 dl water

2 slit vanilla pods

1 tsp grated lime rind

Put the sugar in a saucepan, heat it, stir it and allow it to burn until it is a golden brown. Add the split vanilla pods and water. (Be careful, as water can spit when it comes into contact with hot sugar.)

Cook until it forms a syrup.

Finally add the grated lime rind and cool. Pour onto the berries and mix carefully.

Crème caramel, or flan, has been a popular dessert in Finland for decades now.

Winter Darkness – Christmas Lights

In time the lakes will ice over and you can go skating or skiing. Then it will not be long before preparations have to be made for Christmas. The children will already be looking forward to the arrival of Santa Claus, whose home is in Finnish Lapland.

Christmas is above all a family festival, and the time leading up to it is full of all sorts of things to do: there are presents to make or buy, traditional foods to prepare and lots of baking to be done. Christmas, too, has changed greatly over the years, but one thing that has always been the same is the desire for physical comforts, for good food regardless of the family's means. And the aesthetic side is important, too. Christmas calls for a thorough cleaning of the house, decorations, a beautifully laid table and suitable music.

Red-cheeked apples and prunes are the fruits for Christmas, while the characteristic smells are those of cinnamon, cloves, ginger, orange peel and cardamom, especially in the gingerbread dough. The making of gingerbread and Christmas tarts is fun for all the family, large and small. Home-baked goodies like this also make useful Christmas presents, as does sweet home-made mustard to go with the Christmas ham.

The traditional warming drink for the Christmas season is *glögg*, which has come to us from Sweden. This is a mulled red or white wine that can equally well be made in a non-alcoholic version, from berry juices.

The main meal is eaten on Christmas Eve, but people have learned to spread the celebration over a number of days all told. Breakfast usually takes the form of boiled rice pudding with sugar and cinnamon, and if you are the person in the family who finds the almond in it, this will bring you good luck.

The gingerbread spices – cinnamon, cloves, orange peel and ginger – are among the most homely smells of Christmas.

Christmas foods:

rice porridge, glassmaster's herring, herring salad, herring caviar, mushroom salad, lightly salted salmon, fish roe, stockfish, ham, swede casserole and carrot casserole and rice baked in the oven, sweetened mashed potato baked in the oven, prune kissel, prune and cream parfait, Christmas tarts and ginger biscuits.

A Christmas menu

- Glassmaster's herring, lightly salted salmon, Baltic herrings with mustard dressing, fish roe, mushroom salad, *rosolli*,
- Christmas ham with swede casserole, sweet potato casserole, boiled prunes, tinned peas, home-made mustard
- Prune kissel, or prune and cream parfait or Christmas tarts and whipped cream

Previous spread: The winter scene is at its most beautiful when the sun lends colour to the snowy forests and hill slopes.

Christmas ham

The ham is usually cooked either the preceding day or during the night before Christmas Eve and finished off just before serving.

a salted ham (4–5 kg)

for the crust:

1 egg yolk

2 tbsp mustard

2 tbsp dried breadcrumbs

2 tsp sugar

Dry the ham with a paper towel. Insert an oven thermometer at the thickest point, without touching the bone.

Roast at 100–120°C until the thermometer shows the right temperature for salted ham (75–77°C). Take the ham out of the oven and allow it to cool. Remove the thermometer.

Remove the skin carefully with a pair of scissors and a small, sharp knife, leaving the layer of fat on the meat. Mix the egg yolk and mustard, and spread over the fat. Mix the sugar and breadcrumbs and sprinkle on top of this.

Set the oven temperature to 225–250°C. Return the ham to the oven and bake until the bread-crumbs are slightly browned.

Serve garnished with prunes, peas and slices of cooked apple, accompanied by swede casserole and mustard.

Families differ in their Christmas traditions, but one thing they have in common is the desire to do things "in the same way as before". A salad of chopped salted mushrooms may be a "must" for some families, while others may prefer herring caviar or Baltic herrings in mustard sauce. Very many people insist on herring salad, or the equivalent without the herring, known as *rosolli*, which is also a frequent part of any good buffet table all the year round. Other savouries may include lightly salted salmon, fish roe and smoked fish. Sometimes meat pies, or a thin meat broth may be served between the main meals, or else stockfish, *lipeäkala*, dried cod or haddock softened by soaking in a lye solution, which will usually be accompanied by potatoes and a white béchamel sauce.

It is the ham that traditionally crowns the Christmas meal, and even today every second household will have a ham, although turkey has also become popular in recent years and there are some people who prefer roast lamb, a joint of elk, especially in hunting families, or reindeer, in Lapland. People on some of the islands celebrate with a Christmas pike.

Most households dig out their old recipes just before Christmas, and radio programmes are full of advice on how to cook your ham. The roasting of such a large joint is a significant event in most households, something that happens only once a year. Much discussion usually arises over the dishes that go with it, as well: the sweetened potato and swede casseroles that are also baked in the oven, although the swede casserole, and one made of carrot and rice, can be bought ready-made in the shops.

The best drink to go with the relatively salty parts of the Christmas fare is home-brewed beer or regular beer, while the ham is often accompanied by a good red wine.

The ham crowns the Christmas dinner.

It is as advisable to make the marinaded fish dishes well before Christmas. The contents of these pots include Baltic herrings with mustard dressing and glassmaster's herring.

Baltic herrings with mustard dressing *(sinappisilakat)*

1 kg Baltic herrings,
or 600 g Baltic herring fillets,
sprats or fresh sardines

for the marinade:

5 dl water
2 dl white wine vinegar
2 tsp salt

for the mustard dressing:

3 tbsp mustard, 1/3 of it French mustard
2 tbsp sugar
1 tsp salt
2 tsp white wine vinegar
3/4 dl water
1 dl cooking oil
plenty of chopped dill

Fillet the fish, skinning it if you wish. Cut them in half lengthways.

Mix the marinade and pour it over the fish. Allow to stand for 2–3 hours.

To make the mustard dressing, mix the mustard, sugar, salt, vinegar and water together and add the oil gradually, stirring well.

Drain the fish fillets thoroughly.

Place alternate layers of fish, chopped dill and mustard dressing in a jug or jar. Cover and refrigerate for at least one day before serving.

Serve with boiled or baked potatoes and rye or other dark bread.

Herring caviar *(sillikaviaari)*

Finely chop 1 fillet of salted or matjes herring. 1 hard-boiled egg and a small onion. Mix them together with 1 dl of smetana or crème fraîche and season with 1–2 teaspoonful of sweet mustard. Serve cold with blinis or jacket potatoes.

Glassmaster's herring *(lasimestarinsilli)*

2 salted herrings
water
1 carrot, sliced
1 red onion, peeled and sliced
8 whole allspice
8 whole white peppers
4 whole cloves
1 bay leaf
(1 tbsp mustard seeds)

for the liquid:

2 dl white wine vinegar
2 dl water
1 dl sugar

Soak the herrings for a day in cold water, changing the water a couple of times. Clean the fish and cut the skin away from the underside. Cut into pieces suitable for serving.

Place the pieces of herring in a glass jar in layers together with the onion rings, slices of carrot and spices. Bring the liquid ingredients to the boil and let the mixture cool thoroughly.

Pour the cold liquid over the pieces of herring.

Store in a cold place for two or three days.

Serve with boiled potatoes

Glassmaster's herring, made from fresh herrings

4 fresh herrings

2 carrots

2 red onions

4 bay leaves

2 tbsp pickling condiments

for the liquid:

2 dl white wine vinegar

1 dl sugar

3 tbsp coarse sea salt

Clean the herrings and remove the heads, tails and fins. Open the stomach and rinse quickly with cold water. Cut the fish into 2 cm pieces.

Arrange these pieces in layer in a glass jar, with slices of carrot and red onion, bay laves and the pickling condiments in between.

Bring the liquid to the boil and cool it until it is really cold. Pour it into the jar and store in the cold for at two days before serving.

Mushroom salad

1/2 litre salted mushrooms, soaked and drained

1 small onion

2 dl sour cream or thick cream

ground black pepper or allspice

(lemon juice and a pinch of sugar)

Soak the salted mushrooms in water and very finely chop them and the onion. Whip the cream. Mix the mushrooms with the sour cream or whipped cream. (Season with lemon juice and a pinch of sugar if you wish.)

Pour into a serving dish and sprinkle with ground black pepper or allspice.

Herring salad *(sillisalaatti)*

1 fillet of matjes herring

2 raw beetroots

2 medium-sized carrots

2–3 potatoes

1 cucumber, pickled in brine or vinegar with dill

1 apple

1 small onion

a dash of vinegar

salt and pepper

for placing on top:

1 hard-boiled egg, chopped

Cook the beetroots, carrots and potatoes separately. Peel and dice all the vegetables. Mix the salad ingredients and place on a serving dish. Add salt and pepper.

Cut the herring in pieces.

Serve garnished with hard-boiled egg, parsley and the dressing separately.

A salad of the vegetables alone makes a delicious everyday dish. If it does not have herring in it, it is known as *rosolli*.

Dressing for herring salad or rosolli

2 dl thick cream

2 tsp sugar

1 tsp white wine vinegar

1 tbsp water in which the beetroots were cooked

Whip the cream to a loose froth, mix in the sugar and vinegar, and then add the beetroot water, which will give the dressing its pink colour.

Home-made mustard

2 dl mustard powder

2 dl sugar

3 eggs

2 dl thick cream

(a little salt)

(1 tbsp cognac)

Measure the ingredients out into a small saucepan and mix together well. Heat, stirring all the time, until the mixture begins to thicken.

Be careful, because it burns easily. Take off the heat and season.

This is a sweet mustard and is at its best a few days after it is made. Keep in the fridge.

Sweet potato casserole *(imelletty perunalaatikko)*

1 kg floury potatoes

water for boiling

2 tbsp plain flour

2 tsp salt

about 3 1/2 dl milk, preferably the full-fat variety

1 tbsp melted butter

2 tbsp treacle

Boil the potatoes in their skins. Peel while still hot and mash with an electric whisk (to avoid lumps). While the mashed potatoes are still warm, mix in the flour. Cover the dish with a tea towel and let the mixture stand at room temperature for 3–4 hours or overnight.

Taste the mixture. If it is not sweet enough, add a little sugar. Add the salt, milk, treacle and butter. Mix well.

Grease an ovenproof casserole and pour in the mixture in. Leave space for it to rise as it cooks. Bake for 1–2 hours at 150°C.

Swede casserole *(lanttulaatikko)*

1 large swede or 2 small ones

water, a pinch of salt

1 dl cream

1/2 dl dried breadcrumbs

2 eggs

1/2–1 dl treacle

a little grated nutmeg

some of the water in which the swede was cooked

for the top:

breadcrumbs

Peel and dice the swede. Cook in slightly salted water until soft. When done, drain and mash the swede or put it through a blender.

Let the breadcrumbs swell in the cream and add to the swede. Beat the eggs and add them together with the treacle and nutmeg. Add a little of the cooking liquid if the mixture is too thick.

Grease an ovenproof casserole and pour in the mixture. Pattern the top with a spoon. Sprinkle dry breadcrumbs on top. Bake at 175°C for about an hour.

Rice porridge
(riisipuuro)

2 dl water

2 dl short-grained rice

1 litre full-fat milk

1 tsp salt

Heat the water in a thick-bottomed saucepan and stir in the rice. Cook for a couple of minutes, then add the milk and heat again, stirring regularly, until the pudding comes to the boil. Cook gently for 25–30 minutes, stirring from time to time. Season with salt towards the end of the cooking time.

Note: If you wish, you can hide a whole peeled almond in the pudding, which will bring good luck to the person who finds it.

Prune cream

1 egg

3/4 dl sugar

2 1/2 dl cooked pited prunes, chopped

2 dl thick cream

2 tsp lemon juice

1 tsp vanillin

5 gelatine leaves

(or 1 envelope of unflavoured gelatine powder)

for the topping:

whipped cream, whole or puréed prunes

Soak the gelatine leaves in cold water. Press out the excess water and dissolve the leaves in 1 dl of boiling water. If you are using gelatine powder, follow the directions on the envelope.

Whisk the egg and sugar into a froth. Add the prunes and gelatine mixture, then the lemon juice and vanillin. Whip the cream and fold it into the other ingredients.

Place in a bowl and decorate with whipped cream and whole prunes or spots of puréed prune.

Prune kissel
(luumukiisseli)

250 g pitted prunes

1 litre water

1 cinnamon stick

2 dl sugar

1 dl berry syrup

4 tbsp potato flour + 1 dl cold water

to decorate:

whipped cream

Soak the prunes overnight in a bowl of water.

Pour the contents into a saucepan, add the cinnamon stick and sugar and simmer gently for half an hour. Add the berry syrup.

Dissolve the potato flour in the cold water.

Take the saucepan off the heat and add this thickening in a steady stream, mixing well the whole time. Bring to a boil once more.

Pour into a suitable bowl for serving. Cool.

Serve with whipped cream.

Malt bread
(mallasleipä)

5 dl pure orange juice

2 dl malt (as used for making home-brewed beer)

2 tsp salt

50 g yeast

1 1/2 dl syrup

4 dl rye flour

about 6 dl bread flour

100 g soft butter or margarine

for the surface:

1 1/2 dl water

1 tbsp syrup

Allow the malt to soak in the orange juice for a couple of hours. Crush the yeast and add this together with the salt, syrup, half the flour and the butter or margarine, softened at room temperature. Knead the dough well and leave to rise for about an hour.

Mix the rest of the flour into the dough and shape into two loaves on a floured baking table. Place these loaves on an oven tray and allow to rise again.

Bake at 200°C for about 45 minutes. Brush the tops of the loaves with a mixture of syrup and water when you take them out of the oven.

Christmas tarts
(joulutortut)

for the pastry:

200 g soft butter or margarine

3 dl flour

3/4 dl cold water

1 tsp vinegar

for the filling:

sweetened prune purée or plum jam

for brushing on the surface:

beaten egg

Put all the pastry ingredients into a bowl and mix quickly to a dough by hand. Don't knead the dough too much. Put it in a cold place to harden.

Roll it out on a floured board, folding it a few times to make it into a puff pastry, and finally roll it into a sheet 1/2 cm thick. Cut this sheet into 7 x 7 cm squares. Split the corners of each square. Place a knob of prune purée or plum jam in the middle of each square. Fold over every second split end into the centre to form a windmill-like tart. Brush with beaten egg and bake at 250°C until light brown.

To make semicircular tarts, cut into circles, fill and fold in half. Bake as above. Both types of Christmas tart are popular in Finland.

Making gingerbread biscuits is an important part of Christmas for young bakers.

Parainen ginger biscuits

1 dl dark treacle
1 tsp cinnamon
1 tsp ginger
1 tsp cloves
1 tsp dried orange peel
1 tsp salt
150 g butter or margarine
1 dl sugar
1 egg
1 tsp baking soda
about 6 1/2 dl plain flour

Bring the syrup and spices to the boil. Allow to cool for a while.

Whisk the butter and sugar together, add the warm spice and syrup mixture and the egg. Then add the flour and baking soda and mix to a dough. Let the dough stand overnight in a cold place.

Then roll it out in a sheet 2 mm thick and cut out biscuits with a cutter. Place them on a baking tray and bake in a 225°C oven until a golden brown.

Christmas *glögg*

(FOR 4 SMALL GLASSES)

5 dl blackcurrant juice,
diluted ready to drink
juice and strips of the rind of 1/2 an orange
1 tsp cardamom seeds
4 whole cloves
2 cinnamon sticks
(1 vanilla pod)
sugar
also:
whole blanched almonds
raisins

Peel the half orange with a potato peeler and cut the rind into strips. Squeeze out the juice and put this together with the other ingredients into a saucepan.

Bring to the boil and take off the heat. Add sugar if required. Put the lid on the saucepan and allow to stand for 30 minutes. Pour through a sieve.

Put some almonds and raisins into each glass and pour the hot *glögg* on top. Serve at once.

You can make a more powerful *glögg* if you wish, by adding a dash of *Koskenkorva* or *Finlandia* vodka.

Christmas Is Over

The New Year is ushered in with fireworks and a glass of sparkling wine. Although the days are still dark, we are moving towards lighter times once again. The earth is covered in snow and the lakes have a sheet of ice on them, but something exciting is going on under the ice for those with a gastronomic turn of mind: it is spawning time for the burbot. This is the time to invite your friends and family to eat burbot roe with *blini* pancakes. This light-coloured, fine-grained roe is a great delicacy, and certainly a good reason for holding a party.

Homely flavours:
sausage soup, pea soup and
salmon soup.

Young families may entertain their visitors in a more homely fashion, but for them, too, the winter weekends are a good time for sharing a meal, whether it is soup, a stew or a dish baked in the oven. It is fashionable at the moment for couples to do the cooking together, and the kitchen is a place where everyone can gather. The things to serve after spending some time out of doors are hot berry juice, cocoa or the Christmas hot mulled juice known as *glögg*.

The Finns are hospitable people and are happy to be able to invite visitors to their homes. A family birthday or namesday is always a good cause for celebration, and one important national day is February 5th, when the whole population enjoy the cakes named after the national poet, Johan Ludwig Runeberg (1804–1877) and produced at one time in his home town of Porvoo. These little cakes built up out of cake and biscuit crumbs topped with a ring of sugar icing that has a spot of jam in the centre.

Shrove Tuesday has its own buns, large fluffy ones made out of a wheat dough as used for *pulla* and cut in half and filled with marzipan or jam and

Winter foods:
more substantial soups and sauces,
stews and casseroles,
dishes baked in the oven,
root vegetables,
burbot, Christmas dishes,
shrove Tuesday delicacies,
glögg and hot juices

A winter menu

- Mushroom salad and potatoes
- Karelian stew, vegetables baked in the oven
- Poor knights

Runeberg cakes, the favourite of our national poet.

Runeberg cakes
(Runebergin tortut)

125 g butter or margarine
1 egg
1 dl sugar
1 dl whipping cream
1/2 dl ground almonds
2 dl crushed rusks, ginger biscuits or other biscuits
1 1/2 dl plain flour
1 tsp baking powder

for the icing:

1 tbsp water
about 1 dl icing sugar
about 1 dl raspberry jam

Melt the butter or margarine and cool the liquid fat. Whip the cream to a froth and mix in the ground almonds, crumbs, flour and baking powder.

Beat the eggs and sugar to a light-coloured froth, add the cooled fat and fold in the mixture of crumbs, flour and cream.

Grease a bun tray and divide out the mixture into the individual wells or paper cups, leaving room for the cakes to rise.

Bake for 15–20 minutes at 200°C, then allow to cool.

Mix the icing sugar to a thick paste with the water. Put a spot of jam in the centre of the top of each cake and surround this with icing sugar.

whipped cream. These buns were served in Finland in a bowl with hot milk poured over them, but nowadays they are normally eaten with coffee.

Shrove Tuesday has developed into a day for outdoor activities in Finland, even though in Catholic countries it was originally connected with the beginning of the Lenten fast. Then it was the custom to "stock up" for the period of fasting by eating fatty foods such as smoked pork and sausages. Although pea soup and pancakes are part of our diet all the year round, they are compulsory on Shrove Tuesday.

Soups are the thing for winter meals: meat soup, cabbage soup, sausage soup and game soup made with either elk or reindeer meat, mushroom soup, Borsch soup made from beetroots, salmon or burbot soup and perch or whitefish (lavaret) broth. The soup in a Finnish meal is often so plentiful and so filling that it should be regarded as the main course. You can usually tell a Finnish fish soup by the small drop of milk or cream added to it, and frequently also whole berries of all-spice. On the other hand, the burbot soup made in Kainuu is a clear broth to which melted butter and raw onion are added when eating it.

Casseroles baked in the oven are very popular in winter time, as they are simple, plentiful and practical – typical "slow food". You can even buy these oven-ready in foil dishes and bring them home to warm up. The most common ingredients are cabbage, potatoes, carrot, swede, minced meat and macaroni and minced liver.

The appearance of small holes in the ice on the lakes tells us that the fishing season has begun. Fishing through a hole in the ice is a popular winter pastime, both pleasant and useful, the best catches being of perch, roach, burbot, pike-perch and ruff.

Minced meat and macaroni baked in the oven is a popular everyday dish.

Minced meat and macaroni baked in the oven *(makaronilaatikko)*

4 dl macaroni (or penne)
water, salt
300 g minced meat
1 tbsp rapeseed oil
1 onion
salt, black pepper
1–2 tsp thyme or oregano
for the egg and milk sauce:
3 eggs
6 dl milk
1 tsp salt
for garnishing:
grated cheese

Cook the macaroni in salt water. Pour the water off and rinse the macaroni in cold water.

Peel and chop the onion. Brown the minced meat in the oil, add the chopped onion and seasoning and fry for about five minutes. Mix into the macaroni, and transfer the mixture to a greased oven dish.

Beat the eggs into the milk and season with salt. Pour this mixture over the macaroni and meat in the dish and sprinkle the surface with grated cheese.

Cook in a 175°C oven for about an hour.

Fatty pork in gravy *(läskisoosi)*

100–150 g fresh or smoked belly pork
about 2 tbsp plain flour
1 onion
hot water
salt, white pepper

Cut the pork into slices or cubes and brown in a pan in its own fat. Remove it from the pan and add the flour instead, to brown it.

Add the finely chopped onion and simmer until transparent. Pour in enough boiling water and stir to a smooth sauce.

Return the meat to the pan and simmer until it is cooked.

Season, and add a dash of mustard, ketchup or other condiments if you wish.

Shrove Tuesday buns *(laskiaispullat)*

Form good-sized buns out of a pulla dough (see page 163), bake them, allow them to cool and then cut them in half horizontally.

Fill them with strips of marzipan, and serve in the traditional way, with hot milk in a cereal bowl.

They can also be filled with jam and whipped cream and served with coffee.

Beef and vegetable soup
(lihakeitto)

1 1/4 litres water
1/2 tbsp salt
750 g beef on the bone (breast, shin etc.)
1 onion
8 whole allspice
1 piece of swede
2 carrots
1 piece of celeriac (100 g)
1 piece of parsnip (100 g)
1 small leek
4 potatoes
parsley

Heat the salted water in a large saucepan. When it is lukewarm, add the meat and cook until foam forms on the surface. Skim this off.

Peel and cut all the vegetables into small cubes. Keep the potatoes in cold water. Add the allspice, swede and diced carrots.

Cook until the meat starts to be tender, then add the diced celeriac and parsnip.

When the meat is tender, lift it out onto a chopping board. Cut up the peeled potatoes, slice the leek into rings and add these to the soup.

Separate the meat from the bones, cut it into 2 x 2 cm cubes and put these back into the soup.

Season to taste.

Serve piping hot, garnished with parsley.

Fish soup
(kalakeitto)

1 litre fish stock or water with
a fish stock cube dissolved in it
1 onion
(a piece of leek)
4–6 potatoes
8 whole allspice
about 400 g fillet of salmon, pike-perch,
perch or burbot
(salt)
2 dl cream, or a mixture of cream and milk
2 tbsp plain flour
for garnishing:
dill and chives
butter

Peel the potatoes and cut them into pieces. Peel and finely chop the onion. (Rinse the leek and cut into strips.) Heat the fish stock and add the allspice, potatoes, (leek) and onion, and boil for about 10 minutes.

Cut the fillets of fish into pieces and add them on top of the pieces of potato. Cook with the lid on for about 10 minutes.

Add the flour to the cream or milk and cream mixture and stir into the soup. Cook gently for another 5–10 minutes. Test for salt, then sprinkle with dill and chives. Serve immediately.

Note:

If you use burbot, cut the skinned fish in pieces crosswise and place these on top of the potatoes together with the fish's liver.

Traditional sausage soup
(makkarakeitto)

1 litre beef stock

a large piece of celeriac,
peeled and cut into small cubes (100 g)

1 leek, sliced

1 carrot, peeled and cut into small cubes

5–7 peeled potatoes, diced

4–6 whole allspice

8 or more cooked sausages (e.g. nakki)

parsley

Put the vegetables and allspice into the boiling stock. Simmer for about 10 minutes.

Cut the sausages into 2–3 cm pieces and add to the simmering soup.

Season to taste. Garnish with parsley and serve with rye bread or crispbread and butter.

Note:

Soft, uncooked pork sausages *(siskonmakkarat)* are also used in Finland to make a very popular sausage soup. If using uncooked sausages, add these when the vegetables are almost done, by cutting off the end of the sausage and slowly squeezing 2–3 cm of the contents straight into the soup with your fingers. Cook for another 8 minutes.

Pea soup
(hernekeitto)

1 1/2–2 l water

4 dl dried peas

1/2 kg knuckle of pork (salted),
some smoked, if available

(salt)

8 whole allspice

1 tsp dried marjoram

1–2 tsp mustard

Rinse the peas and soak them overnight in cold water. Cook them in the same water the next day. Add the pork and the spices and cook slowly with the lid on for about 3 hours. When the meat is done, take it out of the saucepan and remove the skin and bone. Cut the meat into cubes and return it to the soup. Add salt if necessary.

Season with mustard and serve hot.

Culinary Moments, on Working Days and at Weekends

Times have also changed with regard to the rhythm of mealtimes in the home. Many families have outside interests that interfere with the time spent together in the afternoons and evenings, and in some ways the most important family meal nowadays is breakfast. Most Finns have become accustomed to various forms of porridge from their infancy, and the selection of these is indeed vast. One of the most popular, even as a school meal, is an oven-baked porridge made of whole hulled grains and eaten with bilberry juice or bilberry soup. Porridge will keep hunger at bay for a long time and serves as a good source of healthy fibres which the human body needs. Often bran is added to the ready-made porridge mixtures, and there may also be muesli, corn flakes and almost always yoghurt or the fermented milk known in Finnish as *viili* on the table as well as milk. In some parts of the country it is common to sprinkle the top of the *viili* with *talkkuna*.

Bread is an essential for the Finnish breakfast table, and most often it is made of whole-grain flour. There are also various margarines or cheese spreads that one can put on bread together with butter or instead of it. Vitamin C can be obtained from fruit juices, fresh fruit, vegetables or berries.

We are constantly faced with choices that we have to make regarding our food, and people tend to look on these choices as befits their age. For older people the preparing of food is a value in its own right, while for younger people savings in time may be all-important. One characteristic of modern eating habits is that they vary over an extremely broad spectrum.

Previous spread:
The best Finnish flavours are those created by traditional methods and with simple combinations of ingredients. Welcome, then, to an early summer meal of small nettle pancakes, nettle pies, spring lettuce, rhubarb juice, rhubarb pie, *viili* with rhubarb jam and flat nettle bread.

The selection of bread varies from one area of the country to another. The breakfast breadbasket at the Tertti Manor House contains Karelian pasties, malt bread, thin crispbread, rye bread and plain yeast bread.

One day we may prepare everything ourselves, from beginning to end, while another day we may buy our food ready-cooked. Ready-prepared meals or ingredients are acceptable, at least on working days, and the demand for these is increasing, although it is also true that their use may be connected with certain stages in life. Even frozen pizza has become a part of everyday life in our times, and mothers no longer feel any need for excuses when they take a ready-made casserole out of the oven onto the table, but feel that they can do so with a clear conscience. The most common ready-made items of all are Karelian pasties, meat balls and various salads.

The companies that specialize in ready-made foods claim to be the guardians of Finnish traditions in this respect, and it is certainly true that some of the dishes that are more laborious to prepare, such as vegetable purées baked in the oven, would probably very seldom be made at home these days. Some, such as *maksalaatikko*, minced liver baked with rice, *makaronilaatikko*, minced meat and macaroni baked in the oven, or *lihaperunalaatikko*, meat and potato casserole, are long-standing favourites, but the present generation of children are able to acquire a taste for them largely because they can be bought ready-made. These, together with cabbage rolls, meat balls and the whipped lingonberry and semolina pudding known as *vispipuuro* are good examples of traditional recipes that have proved successful in our modern times, and all of them have been available commercially for more than 50 years now.

Family meals are mainly weekend events for most people. Then there may be time to make food together, and it is increasingly common for the head of the household and the children to be involved in this. Men began venturing into the kitchen in the

Pearl barley can be cooked in the oven overnight to make a soft, smooth breakfast porridge.

Pearl barley porridge cooked in the oven *(uuniohrapuuro)*

2 dl pearl barley
3 dl cold water
1 1/2 tsp salt
1 litre full-fat milk
knobs of butter for the surface of the porridge and butter to grease the dish

Begin making the porridge the evening before you plan to serve it. Grease an oven dish, measure the pearl barley, water and salt into it and allow to soak for a few hours. Add the milk and a few knobs of butter.

Set the oven temperature at 100°C, put the porridge in the oven and allow to cook for 8–10 hours overnight. If the surface browns too quickly, cover it with aluminium foil.

Serve with sugar, cinnamon and cold milk or berries.

1950s, and children have begun learning cookery at school, where domestic science is a compulsory subject and the boys and girls work together in the home economics classroom. Cooking has become a hobby for the whole family in many cases, and home baking is very much in fashion.

Good, healthy meals

Healthy eating habits are all the rage in works' canteens and school dining rooms, where more fruit and vegetables are to be had than ever before. Attempts are made at schools and at home to follow the recommendations for a high proportion of grain products, potatoes and vegetables. Half a kilo of fruit and vegetables a day is the message, and those people who eat by themselves or in a restaurant or fast food bar at lunch time will fill out their meal with salad, vegetables or fruit.

Free school meals are taken for granted in Finland today, just as the country was a pioneer of this principle in earlier times. Warm, nutritious meals have been served free of charge in Finnish schools for more than 60 years now, having been introduced under a law passed in 1948 to ensure that schoolchildren received at least one hot meal a day that was sufficient to meet 1/3 of their daily energy requirement. The children also receive either milk or soured milk, *piimä*, and bread, either wholemeal bread or crispbread, with their meal.

The schoolchildren themselves have to provide any other snacks that they need during the school day, and as the consumption of sweets and lemonade has been on the increase, the food industry has now begun to develop more healthy alternatives, muesli bars, yoghurts, sandwiches and small portions of food that can be heated in a microwave oven.

Functional foodstuffs

People in Finland have always made use of functional foodstuffs, i.e. foods that have a beneficial effect on health, as whole-grain products based on rye, barley and oats have been a part of the staple diet. Nowadays it is also common to use more healthy vegetable oils and fats in cooking.

And the emergence of new, precisely targeted functional foods continues. The most Finnish of these are inevitably rye and oats, which have been proved scientifically to promote well-being by reducing the incidence of vascular diseases and lowering cholesterol levels. Another product that has gained an international reputation for beneficial effects on blood cholesterol is the Benecol margarine containing vegetable stanols. This has now been accompanied on the market by yoghurts, milk, snack bars, chicken meat balls and salads that all have stanols in them. High quality cold-pressed rapeseed oil is also produced in Finland, and cooking oil from gold-of-pleasure seeds (*Camelina sp.*).

Many people finish their meal by popping a piece of xylitol chewing gum in their mouth. This is an accepted and even recommended habit, as researchers at the University of Turku demonstrated in the 1970s that this sugar extracted from birch reduces the incidence of dental caries. Another outcome of cooperation between university researchers and the food industry is the probiotic preparation from oats marketed under the name of Yosa.

The Gefilus culture, promoted as "rescue bacteria" capable of putting the whole body in order, is available in milk, soured milk and yoghurt products and in fruit juices.

Yosa, a probiotic preparation from oats, has emerged as a popular health food product.

At Market Places and on Street Corners

Practically every town has its own square where markets are held all the year round, on warm summer days and in the depths of winter, even at -40°C. These markets are like open-air department stores, shop windows for small producers and the places where you can be most certain of finding local specialities. The main reason for going there, though, is the atmosphere. "I'll see you at the market," is a common greeting to be heard at weekends, as the market is always worth a visit, if only for meeting people. The stallholders are still referred to affectionately as the "old women of the market", even though they are mostly pretty young girls nowadays, especially in summer.

There are less things on sale in the market in winter: mostly fish, either fresh or smoked, and otherwise mainly potatoes, brooms, birch whisks for use in sauna, woollen socks and wicker baskets. There are often Karelian pasties and the *kalakukko* fish pies on sale from vans or at separate stalls, and perhaps a tent where you can buy a hot drink. Complete strangers will be packed into this warm shelter side by side, coffee or teacup in hand together with a plate containing a warm meat pie, or the most popular of all, a sugary jam doughnut.

The vast selection of goods in the market in summer varies according to what is in season, progressing from bedding plants for the garden through early vegetables and potatoes to peas and the various cultivated and wild berries, ending up with mushrooms. Bread, cakes and souvenirs are to be had all the time, of course.

July is strawberry time!

In summer you can eat a whole meal at the market place if you wish. You can usually find soup, meat or fish burgers, fried fish (usually vendace) and paella. Cooks from different lands and cultures add colour to the scene, and you can easily find a wok meal to take away.

The market usually begins early in the morning, normally at 7.00 a.m. and the stallholders are ready to pack their things and go home by 2.00 p.m., although there are often evening markets as well in the summer time.

An alternative place to buy similar products in most towns is the covered market hall. These have often gained small restaurants nowadays, frequently using the fresh vegetables, meat and fish sold on the nearby stalls. These are places where you can grab a quick bowl of soup or portion of sushi if you are in a hurry.

Most places also have special market days, when the market square is busier than ever, with more stalls and a greater variety of goods from small producers, ranging from underwear to carpets. Baltic herring markets are held in the coastal towns every autumn, when people from the islands come to sell their fish preserved and spiced in a variety of ways. Salted Baltic herrings, the only true ingredients for a herring casserole baked in the oven, are gradually giving way to newer products.

Most towns also have kiosks in the streets where you can buy sausages, hot dogs and the like. Particularly irresistible, although full of fat, are the deep-fried pies with meat or rice in them. If you are feeling hungry at night you can enjoy a pie filled with egg and sausage, for instance, and if you ask for your pie or hot dog "with all the trimmings" it will be split in half and filled with ketchup, mustard, chopped onions and cucumber relish.

The town of Savonlinna has its own flattened deep-fried doughnuts known as *lörtsyt*, made from a yeast dough and filled with jam or apple purée.

Top of the list in the local markets in June and July are new potatoes, young carrots, green peas in their pods and small turnips.

AKEA HERNE
SUOMI
€/Litra
SIPULI
NIPPU
Uusi PERUNA
SUOMI
3
€/LTR

Travelling Means Eating

Filling stations have taken on a new role these days, as there are many villages where the cafés and village bars have had to close and one popular place where people can meet their friends is often the local garage if it has a café or restaurant. These have indeed become multipurpose institutions in many cases, and may include several shops selling everything from food to souvenirs, beer and wines.

Modern times have also brought with them rural shops established beside the main trunk roads where local small-scale producers are able to sell their foodstuffs and handicrafts, which are looked on as something special relative to the mass-produced goods available elsewhere. These can include flour and other grain products from one or more farms, bread, rusks, pies or cakes baked by local housewives and fresh vegetables, potatoes straight from the ground, cultivated and wild berries, home-made jams and juices, local honey and flowers. The larger sales outlets of this kind may have refrigerators, so that they can sell cheeses, sliced meats, sausages and both smoked and fresh meat. If you are lucky, the producers themselves may be able to tell you how the "guaranteed fresh ham" enjoyed nosing about in its pen and feeding on the barley, oats and hay from the neighbouring fields during its recent life as a pig, and you may equally well meet the person responsible for making the cheese or sausages.

Cinnamon buns *(korvapuustit)*

Dough:

As for pulla, see above. (page 163)

for the filling:

melted or soft butter

ground cinnamon

sugar

1 egg for brushing

Use the same recipe as for coffee bread, but roll the dough into a sheet about 1 cm thick and spread this with a thick layer of melted or very soft butter. Then sprinkle with sugar and cinnamon. If you like, you can add a layer of chopped or ground almonds or other nuts. Roll and cut into slices about 3–5 cm thick. Arrange these on an oven tray covered with greaseproof paper. Allow to rise.

Make a vertical depression in the top of each bun with one finger or with the handle of a knife, so that the spiral-like filling bulges out on both sides.

Let the buns rise further, and then brush with beaten egg and bake at 225°C for 8–10 minutes.

Cinnamon buns are made with plenty of butter and sugar.

In a Finnish Restaurant

In addition to the fact that the majority of Finnish people have one meal a day in a works' canteen, school refectory, lunch bar, café or filling station restaurant, it is common to go out to a restaurant to eat, drink, do business, attend receptions or gourmandize. The newer restaurants are stylishly and invitingly furnished and their bars comfortable and attractive. Many of them serve food even outside regular eating hours, although there are also many high-class "fine dining" restaurants that are open only in the evenings. As elsewhere in the world, it is necessary to check a restaurant's opening times and preferably book a table in advance.

Although Finnish and Scandinavian food is regarded as trendy in the restaurant world, as is organic and locally produced food, it is actually difficult to find distinctly Finnish food other than on the lunch menus of the more conventional restaurants and at places that specialize in Finnish specialities. More often one finds flavours from all over the world mingling together on one's plate. There are admittedly some everyday dishes that have become hits in recent times, such as Baltic herrings, *lapskaus*, cabbage rolls and salmon soup. The recent HelsinkiMenu project has successfully induced about 30 restaurants in the capital to serve a variety of specifically Finnish foods alongside their usually varying menu. The seasons of the year are also reflected in these foods. Summer is obviously the high point for the Finns gastronomically, but magnificent flavours are available at other seasons, too. Traditional ingredients can take on a new guise in the hands of a skilful chef, and it is no longer necessary to resort to enormous amounts of cream and butter.

The Savoy Restaurant in Helsinki, which is now over 70 years old, is a creation of the world-famous Finnish architect Alvar Aalto. Its interior has been delicately restored in its original form and its classic dishes include vorschmack, which is made of minced roast lamb.

Manor Houses and Buffet Tables

Many manor houses and large Finnish country houses have opened their doors to visitors, allowing them to sense the atmosphere of such places and wine and dine in the manner of gentlefolk. The menu usually features both traditional and modern dishes.

The Tertti Manor House near Mikkeli, opened in 1978, is an excellent example of a stylishly managed restaurant that operates on a buffet table principle and also has hotel rooms attached. Going in through the old porch, one immediately finds the décor inside just as elegant as the well-tended courtyard outside. Practically everything is just as it used to be, and the old-world atmosphere is emphasized by the brick-red wallpaper and the pictures telling of the history of the estate.

Although the house is open all the year round, the summer is its busiest time. Then the Finnish buffet table is laid every day of the week with delicious

The best places for sampling Finnish buffet tables and local specialities are farm or manor house restaurants in the country. One such restaurant is that of the Tertti Manor House near Mikkeli, which serves modern à la carte dishes as well as having a magnificent buffet table.

dishes typical of the province of Savo, as correct in style and worthy of a manor house as the furnishings. There are vendace from Kuopio, served either salted or in a vinegar marinade, fresh cheese made of soured milk, flat, unleavened bread baked from potato flour, home-made rye bread, and the house's own crispbread. Fish and game pâtés, salted fish, *rosolli* and mushroom salad are likewise all standard items. The family are especially proud of their rye bread, which is baked using a leaven that has been kept alive for more than a hundred years.

The staff of 8–10 persons includes young waitress in the costumes used by serving girls in olden days, and the house has its own gardener, so that most of the strawberries, currants, raspberries, herbs and vegetables are from its own grounds. These, of course, tend to vary with the seasons, as does the choice of hot dishes.

Once the buffet lunch is over for the day, attention is turned to the carefully prepared *à la carte* menu, which allows the chefs to conjure up wonderful portions from the local lake fish, meat and game. All the food is prepared in the house's own kitchens and immaculately and tastefully served. The wine list is also splendid, and an extra speciality is a non-alcoholic drink made out of blackcurrant leaves from the estate's gardens. The traditional drinks to accompany a buffet meal of this kind are nevertheless beer and a glass of schnapps, the master of the house, Matti Pylkkänen, explains, adding that he very much hopes that the old schnapps custom will survive.

You can also call in at Tertti for coffee and sample its selection of cakes, pastries, S-shaped cinnamon biscuits, rhubarb or bilberry pies, bilberry buns, strawberry gateaux, etc.

Come back as many times as you wish. It is up to you what you take, in what order and how much.

- The first course will normally be fish: herring, Baltic herring, vendace, lightly salted fish, smoked fish – usually whitefish or salmon – and sometimes also fish roe, boiled potatoes and bread.
- The second course may include lampreys, prawns, eel, jellied fish, *rosolli,* fresh cheese and salad.
- The third course will probably contain meat such as ham, reindeer meat, sausages, cold roast beef, smoked lamb, jellied meat, pâtés, terrines and tongue. Try pickled vegetables with these.
- By the fourth course it is time to try small portions of the warm dishes: meat balls, sausages, Jansson's temptation or an omelette.
- The fifth course is the real warm food: roast beef, meat stew or fish.
- The sixth course will be cheese or dessert
- The seventh course can be coffee and cream cake.

Salmon is a must for every buffet table. The grilled skin from ice-cellar or lightly salted salmon is a special delicacy.

Herring and crispbread is a new, attractive way to serve salted and marinaded fish.

Eggs filled with fish roe, herring or cold-smoked salmon

Cut hard-boiled eggs in two and place on a bed of lettuce in a serving dish.
Decorate with dabs of fish roe or pieces of herring or cold-smoked salmon.
Sprinkle with dill or chives.

Cucumber salad

1 large cucumber
1 tsp salt
2 tbsp sugar
for the marinade:
1/2 dl white wine vinegar
1/4 dl water
chopped dill

Rinse the cucumber and cut it into thin slices. Put into a deep dish and sprinkle with salt and sugar. Cover with another dish and shake the slices between the two until they are almost transparent. Mix the water and vinegar. Pour over the cucumber slices. Sprinkle with chopped dill. Keep in a cool place if not to be served immediately.

Herring and crispbread

150–200 g fillet of matjes spiced herring
a medium-sized red onion (50 g)
1 1/2 dl whipping cream
small pieces of crispbread (30 g)

Drain the herring fillet and cut it into good-sized pieces. Peel the onion and cut into small cubes. Whip the cream to a loose froth and carefully mix all the ingredients together.
Serve at once.

Ice-cellar salmon and crisp-fried salmon-skin rolls

1/2 kg salmon
for the salt solution:
1 litre water
1 dl coarse sea salt (100 g)
a good 1/2 dl granulated sugar (60 g)
1 tsp dill seed (2 g)

Bring the water to the boil, add the salt, sugar and dill seed. Bring to the boil again and then cool until cold. Place a boneless fillet of salmon in a deep oven dish, skin upwards, and pour the salt solution over it so that it is entirely covered. Allow to stand in the cold for at least 24 hours, then take the fish out of the solution and dab it dry with kitchen paper before slicing. Cut the salmon into slices leaving a layer of fish about 1/2 cm thick on the skin. Store the slices in the cold.

Crisp-fried salmon-skin rolls:

Heat a cast iron frying pan to a high temperature. Cut the skin into large pieces that will fit into the pan. Fry them in the pan, first with the skin downwards, until it is well browned, and then on the other side. Allow to cool and lift out onto greaseproof paper. Roll each piece up with the help of the paper.
Keep in a fridge until it is time to serve the dish, then cut each roll into slices about 1 cm thick and use as a garnish and accompaniment for the lightly salted salmon.

The fruit and vegetable garden and the flower gardens that have been developed in the ruins of the old cattle barn are now tended by a professional gardener, and the house also has a food shop where you can buy jellies, preserves, spices, sweets, juices and bread, all made according to the manor house's traditional recipes. Another good souvenir to take home if you are a gardener yourself is a cutting of the original Tertti rose.

Delights of the smörgåsbord

A buffet table is the best way of serving a large number of guests at once, as it allows them to choose and fetch their food themselves, and although versions of this system are to be found all over the world, perhaps the best known is the Scandinavian *smörgåsbord*, or *voileipäpöytä*, which will normally provide an ample selection of both cold and hot foods. All the foods, from starters to desserts, are normally set out at the same time, and the temptations are enormous, as there are so many different things to try. The whole idea, however, is to take your time and go systematically through all the varieties of food that appeal to you. You can go round the table as many times as you like.

Times have admittedly changed, and a really sumptuous *smörgåsbord* is a rarity these days. Some of the most plentiful are those to be found on the ships plying between Finland, Sweden and Estonia, whereas the buffet tables at filling stations, which do not even lay claim to this name, are a cheap version in which you can eat as much as you can at a fixed price. In between these extremes we find the buffet table as set out for celebrations or in traditional local restaurants, where the foods on offer may be of a restricted or local kind.

Wildfowl terrine

400 g pheasant and/or breast and leg of goose, off the bone
300 g fatty pork
100 g red onion
50 g potato
2 dl strong wildfowl or meat broth
1 tsp fresh rosemary leaves
1 tbsp strong sweet mustard
salt and black pepper
1 tbsp blackcurrant jelly
1/2 dl thick cream

Peel the red onion and potato, cut them into pieces and put them in a saucepan. Add the broth, rosemary and other seasoning and the blackcurrant jelly.

Cook until the pieces of potato and onion are done and the liquid has evaporated. Cool.

Pass the mixture through a mincer, and mince the meat separately. Combine the two and add the cream. Mix well. Fry a test sample of the mixture and check for taste. Store in the cold for about 12 hours.

Line a long, narrow 1-litre dish with a sufficiently large sheet of damp greaseproof paper that some hangs over the side. Fill the dish with the mixture and turn the edges of the paper inwards to cover it.

Cook in a 150°C oven for about an hour. Cool, turn out onto a plate and cut into slices when cold. Serve with blackcurrant jelly.

The manor house dishes display influences from both east and west. This is a wildfowl terrine, Tertti style.

Crown your meal with dessert

When the first cultivated and wild berries ripen all you can do is pop them straight into your mouth or bring them to someone else hidden in the palm of your hand or threaded on a stalk of grass. Berries are at their most delicious just like that. There are other things that you can do with them, though. You can mix them into salads, boil them into kissel or use them in desserts. Travellers may find themselves being served with frozen berries, raspberries, lingonberries or cranberries, topped with hot toffee sauce, or with hot *leipäjuusto*, "bread cheese", and cloudberries.

"Ice cream with jam" was a well-loved favourite in earlier times, but now the jam often has to give way to fresh berries or fruit. Although the consumption of ice cream in Finland is remarkably evenly distributed through the year, there is a peak in summer, when ice cream can also be bought at kiosks. The most popular flavours are those of the local berries, such as strawberry or cranberry, the Finnish apples that have a tinge of cinnamon in them, or chocolate, of course. Young people also like to use strawberries, bilberries or raspberries in milk shakes or smoothies, or to mix them into quark or yoghurt.

Pancakes with sugar or jam on them taste just as wonderful as everyday fare as they do at a party, and the best of all are pancakes made of a mixture of wheat and barley flour and cooked on a cast-iron grill pan, a modern barbeque accessory rather akin to a wok, based on the shape of the bottom of an iron cauldron.

One nostalgic taste is that of cheese made in the oven out of the first milk from a cow after calving, especially when it has sugar and cinnamon sprinkled on the top and is served with cold milk.

One of the old-time winter favourites that has survived is the pink, fluffy mixture of semolina and

The best of all desserts in summer is simply a dish of fresh wild berries eaten on their own or with cream, yoghurt, *viili* or ice cream.

Poor knights *(köyhät ritarit)*

a slice of white toast bread or coffee bread (pulla) per person
1 egg
3 dl milk
a pinch of salt
for frying:
butter or margarine
for the topping:
lingonberry, raspberry or strawberry jam
(whipped cream)

Cut a thick slice of bread for each person. Whisk the egg and mix in the milk and a pinch of salt. Dip the slices of bread in the milk and egg mixture and fry until a golden brown on both sides. Serve hot with jam on. Top it off with whipped cream to make your "poor knights" into "rich knights".

Pancakes

1/2 l milk

(or 2 1/2 dl cream and

2 1/2 dl water or mineral water)

2 1/2 dl plain flour

about 1 tsp salt

2 eggs

(1 tbsp sugar)

Mix the flour and milk, add the salt and beat in the eggs. Let the batter stand for a minute before frying. Fry the pancakes in a hot pan greased with butter or margarine. Serve with jam.

To make a single large pancake from the same batter, pour into a greased oven tray and bake at 225°C until a golden brown (10–15 minutes).

berries known as *vispipuuro*, which can also be bought ready-made in the shops. Fruit pies and crumbles are made with jam or purée in the winter, but with fresh berries in summer. The first filling to come into season is rhubarb, which can be turned into delicious desserts by skilful hands. *Pappilan hätävara*, the "vicarage standby", follows the same idea as English trifle or the Italian *zuppa inglese*, a delicious dessert that can be made out of simple ingredients in an emergency, and *köyhät ritarit*, "poor knights", are the same thing as French Toast.

The list of other popular desserts includes caramel puddings, baked Alaska, fruit parfaits, Charlotte Russe and the many fine chocolate dishes that are familiar from the old cookery books. You can also try Finnish halva, elegant pastries or home-made biscuits with your coffee, for instance.

Pancakes are a good meal or dessert all the year round. The right drink to enjoy with them is cold milk.

Enjoy Your Coffee

The life of the Finns revolves around coffee. People have a fixed daily coffee-drinking rhythm, which usually means coffee for breakfast whether they are on holiday or at work. Nowadays it is mostly the product of modern coffeemakers, although a great deal more use is made of the traditional copper coffee pot in summer.

Finland heads the world statistics for the consumption of coffee, so that most people regard events in the coffee-producing countries of the world as matters of crucial importance. The average annual consumption of 9.8 kilos of coffee per person is the equivalent of 4 or 5 cups a day, although tea is increasing in popularity. Another recent trend has been for the lightly roasted Finnish coffee to give way to dark roasts or spiced coffees, sometimes drunk continental-style from a glass, often with milk. Thus a new coffee-house culture has spread throughout the country.

"Let's go for a coffee!" or "Will you have a cup of coffee?" can be heard here as often as "Let's have a nice cup of tea" in England, and the statutory pauses at work are known, naturally, as "coffee breaks". Libraries, theatres and hairdressers will usually have their own coffee bars.

The usual thing to eat with coffee during the day is still *pulla*, a sweet bun made of wheat flour. The eternal favourites are a large, fluffy bun spiced with cinnamon and sugar, known as *korvapuusti*, a "box on the ear", or else Danish pastries, known to the Finns as wienerbröd, or simply *viineri*. Sugar and artificial sweetener are equally acceptable in your coffee nowadays, and cream is frequently replaced by a lighter alternative, ordinary milk.

The rich selection of sweet cakes and biscuits includes berry muffins and home-made biscuits.

A homely coffee party

Small mushroom pasties

Korvapuusti buns

Tosca cake

Fruit pie or cream cake

Coffee is frequently drunk from mugs at breakfast and at work, but proper coffee cups have not yet been consigned to museums, even though the village of Posio in Lapland does have an International Coffee Cup Museum. The coffee table for a formal celebration will still be laid with elegant cups, saucers and plates in the traditional style – regardless of the fact that the younger guests may not always know what they are supposed to do with a saucer!

One inspired Finnish invention of recent times has been Kahwa, a soft drink made from the red flesh surrounding raw coffee beans.

A traditional coffee party

Invitations to coffee are an important part of the Finnish culture, and it is in the form of a coffee party that most birthdays, namesdays, weddings, funerals and other important functions are celebrated. Although it is becoming more common to entrust the arranging of these events to outside caterers, something home-made or local is usually included among the cakes and pastries on offer. Times have changed, however, in this respect, too. It used to be a point of etiquette to serve "seven sorts" of accompaniment to coffee, mostly cakes, home-made biscuits, pastries and, to crown them all, a cream cake. The centrepiece would often be an ornate ring of *pulla*, freshly made and smelling deliciously of cardamom, with the space in the centre filled with home-made S-shaped cinnamon biscuits, almond rings, sandwich biscuits, oatmeal crisps and ginger biscuits. The more strands of *pulla* dough were woven together in the ring, the finer it was considered to be! If actual "food" was called for,

Small mushroom pasties

ready-made shortcrust or flaky pastry

for the filling:

200 g fresh mushrooms (champignons, shiitake, ceps, funnel chanterelles or yellow chanterelles)

cooking oil, butter or margarine

1 onion, or 2 spring onions

(1/2 tsp chilli powder)

salt, black pepper or 1–2 tsp soy sauce

1/2 tsp thyme

1 – 2 tbsp crème fraîche

for brushing:

a beaten egg

First prepare the filling. Finely chop the mushrooms and onion. Put some fat in a frying pan and fry the mushrooms for 5 minutes over a steady heat. Add the onion and seasoning and fry for another 5 minutes. Finally add the crème fraîche, which can be brought to the boil.

Roll out the pastry to a sheet about 1/2 cm thick and cut into circles of diameter 8 cm or into squares of approximately the same size.

Place about a tablespoonful of the filling in the centre of each piece of pastry and fold the pastry over it. Shape the pasties into triangles or half-moons, place them on an oven tray and brush them with beaten egg. Bake for a good 5 minutes in a 225°C oven until a beautiful brown in colour.

Tosca cake
(toskakakku)

2 eggs
2 dl granulated sugar
50 g melted butter or margarine
2 dl plain flour
2 tsp baking powder
1 dl cream
for the icing:
100 g butter or margarine
1 dl sugar
100 g flaked almonds
1 1/2 tbsp cream
2 tbsp plain flour

Beat the eggs and sugar to a froth and add the melted butter. Add the baking powder to the flour and stir into the mixture. Finally add the cream.

Pour into a smooth-bottomed greased and breadcrumbed cake tin and bake for about 40 minutes in a 200°C oven. Cover with aluminium foil about halfway through this baking time to prevent the cake from browning too much.

Prepare the icing while the cake is in the oven. Mix the ingredients together and bring to the boil. Spread the icing mixture on the cake and return it to the oven for a further 5–10 minutes, until the icing has turned a beautiful brown.

this usually consisted of small open sandwiches or a sandwich loaf.

Nowadays a coffee party is more likely to feature something that is a cross between a coffee table and a buffet lunch, with more small savoury items and salads to be had. Pride of place is given to local varieties of bread and pies, and alongside the usual fare it is not uncommon to find pizza, sushi or tapas. A fine sight on the table is a sandwich loaf, *voileipäkakku*, made of slices of white or brown bread interleaved with layers of fish, meat or vegetable paste and decorated with fruit, sometimes so beautifully that it is unclear whether it is intended to be savoury or sweet. Sometimes there is also bread with sliced meat, cheeses and pâtés, or savoury quiches filled with ham, cheese, fish, vegetables or mushrooms.

Popular cakes for a coffee table now include cheesecake, plain or flavoured with soft fruit or chocolate, but pride of place still goes to the cream cake, laced with fruit juice to make it soft to suit the Finnish palate and at its most splendid when decorated with fresh summer berries. Local patisseries preserve their skills and customs acquired from Russia, Switzerland or France, and many people prefer to buy a superb, ready-made cake and professionally produced pastries and biscuits.

Home Baking

The smell of pulla

For many people the smell of *pulla* is one of their finest childhood memories. A glass of milk and a fresh sweet bun, whether home-made, brought straight from the bakery or baked from oven-ready frozen buns, is an experience that is passed on from one generation to the next in Finnish homes, and one of the key factors behind that smell is the use of cardamom.

Coffee and *pulla* is part of the daily rhythm of life, and an essential feature of many visits to friends and neighbours.

The dough itself is a versatile raw material that can be served up in many guises: little round buns, rings, *korvapuusti* (large fluffy buns with sugar and cinnamon), Boston cake or fruit tarts, or doughnuts, plain or filled with jam or apple purée and cooked in oil.

Pasties and pies for all tastes

"Press them into little waves, not high crests, as they'll singe on the top." This is the advice mothers give to their daughters about shaping Karelian pasties, which, like Karelian stew, are a traditional food that has now caught on all over Finland.

The Karelian pasty tradition is preserved best in the province of Northern Karelia, where the skill of making them is passed down in the family. By far the best pasties are made at home, as the factory-made equivalents are quite different, being much thicker. The usual filling is boiled rice, although mashed potato or barley can also be used. The dough for the crusts is made of rye flour, water and salt and is then

The smell of *pulla* in the oven has a nostalgic air about it. Large loaves of *pulla* are often plaited.

rolled out with a specially shaped rolling pin that is still an essential today, although some clever people have discovered that you can equally well use a pasta maker for this. After baking in a hot oven, the pasties are brushed with butter. They are normally eaten with egg butter, and sometimes also slices of fish or meat, smoked reindeer, lightly salted whitefish or salmon, or cold-smoked salmon. The small, circular pasties called *rönttöset* that are made in Kainuu are closely related to Karelian pasties but can be filled with a variety of things: vegetables as well as potatoes, and often berries, mainly lingonberries or bilberries.

The crusts for salmon, cabbage, ham, vegetable or mushroom pies can be made of either puff pastry, shortcrust pastry or a yeast dough, and a similar crust filled with minced meat can be spread over a whole baking tray to produce a pie for eating at Christmas or on other festive occasions. The same fillings with puff pastry are also used for small bite-sized pies to serve with coffee. The Karelian *vatruskat* are small pies with a soft crust made with potato flour and wheat flour and have a filling of rice mixed with finely chopped wild mushrooms, while *rastikaiset* are fish pies with a crust of puff pastry.

The selection of fruit pies, baked with shortcrust pastry or *pulla* dough, tends to vary with the season. It is easy when baking *pulla* to set some of the dough aside to fill with jam, fruit purée or whole berries, fresh or frozen, or even quark, for that matter. More tasty fillings can be made from fresh berries in spring, summer and autumn, whereas in winter one has to fall back on frozen ones. The talking-point of the berry-picking season from one year to the next is always what the crust of a bilberry pie should be made of: *pulla* dough or shortcrust pastry?

Finnish doughnuts come in all shapes and sizes, but the word *donitsi* applies to a ring-shaped one.

Coffee bread
(pulla)

2 1/2 dl milk

25 g fresh yeast, or 11 g of dried yeast

1 egg

1 tsp salt

1 dl sugar

1/2 tbsp crushed cardamom

about 1/2 kg flour

100 g butter or margarine

Dissolve the yeast in lukewarm milk, beat the egg and add this to the liquid. Mix in the salt, sugar, cardamom and flour and beat well. If you use dried yeast, add it with the flour.

Soften the butter or margarine and add it to the other ingredients. Knead the dough until it separates easily from the sides of the bowl. Let the dough stand and rise at room temperature for about half an hour. Then form into small rolls or long loaves. Allow these to rise again.

The bread is ready for the oven when you can press the surface down and it immediately the bounces back. Brush with beaten egg.

Bake loaves at 200°C for 20–25 minutes and rolls at 225°C for 5–10 minutes.

"Butter-eye" rolls
(voisilmäpullat)

Form the same coffee bread dough into little rolls and let them rise. Brush with beaten egg.

Make a hole in each with one finger, pressing all the way down to the bottom of the roll. Put 1 tsp butter into each hole. Sprinkle with sugar (and vanillin if desired).

Bake at 225°C for 10–15 minutes.

Finnish doughnuts
(munkit)

Make the same dough as for coffee bread, but use slightly less flour. Form into small rolls and let them rise, covered with a cloth or cling foil.

Cook the doughnuts in hot vegetable oil or coconut oil (180°C) for about 15 minutes, depending on size, or until golden brown.

Drain them on kitchen paper. Roll them in sugar while still warm.

Quick doughnuts

5 dl flour

1/2 dl sugar

1 tsp salt

3 tsp baking powder

2 tsp cardamom

3 dl light cream or top of the milk

2 eggs

Mix the dry ingredients in a bowl and add the milk or cream and eggs. Mix to a smooth dough.

Take small knobs of dough and drop them immediately into hot oil (180°C). Cook until a light brown, about 4–5 minutes.

Roll them in sugar while still warm and serve as soon as possible.

Bilberry roses

(TO MAKE 6 LARGE ROSES OR 12 SMALL ONES)

125 g butter

6 dl plain flour (450 g)

3 tsp baking powder

100 g brown sugar

1 tsp vanilla sugar

2–3 dl fresh bilberries (150 g)

2 eggs

2 1/2 dl milk

Melt the butter and allow it to cool. Sieve the flour and baking powder into a broad, shallow bowl and mix in the sugar, vanilla sugar and bilberries. Make a hollow in the middle of the mixture.

Beat the eggs and milk together, pour the mixture into the hollow and add the butter.

Stir with a wooden spoon until an even dough is obtained. Divide this dough out into greased 1–2 dl bun tins or into the 12 hollows of a bun tray. Bake for 30 minutes at 200°C. Allow to stand in the tins for a moment before taking them out to serve. Dust with icing sugar.

Date cake

200 g	*stoneless dates*
2 dl	*water*
200 g	*butter or margarine*
1 1/2 dl	*sugar*
2	*eggs*
3 dl	*plain flour*
2 tsp	*baking powder*
2 tsp	*vanilla sugar*

for the cake tin:

butter or margarine

breadcrumbs

Heat the oven to 175°C. Grease a large round or elongated cake tin and line it with breadcrumbs.

Cut the dates into pieces and put them in a saucepan with the water. Cook and stir until the mixture is thick and the dates soft. Cool.

Beat the butter or margarine and sugar together to a froth. Add the eggs one at a time, beating well. Add the dates and finally the flour, baking powder and vanilla sugar, all mixed together.

Pour into the cake tin and bake in the lower part of the oven for about an hour.

Cool well before turning out.

Traditional Finnish sandwich biscuits *(herrasväen pikkuleivät)*

150 g butter

1 1/2 dl granulated sugar

1 egg

3 dl plain flour

1 tsp baking powder

1 1/2 tsp vanilla sugar

for sprinkling on the surface:

caster sugar

for the filling:

raspberry jam

Beat the butter and sugar to a froth and beat in the egg. Mix the dry ingredients together and add them to the mixture, stirring well to obtain an even dough. Put the dough on one side in the cold to cool down for a few hours.

Then roll the dough out to a sheet about half a centimetre thick on a floured surface and cut circles from it about the size of a small biscuit. Put these on an oven tray and bake them in a 175°C oven for about 10 minutes. Allow to cool, spread the biscuits with a little raspberry jam and stick them together in pairs. Roll each pair in caster sugar.

A summer coffee table.

Flower herb cake
(kukkaisyrttikakku)

250 g butter

2 1/2 dl sugar

3 eggs

2 dl plain flour

2 dl potato flour

2 tsp baking powder

1/2 dl herbal sugar (from Tertti Manor House)

1/2 dl Triple Sec, Cointreau or Grand Marnier liqueur

Beat the butter and sugar to a froth and beat in the eggs one by one. Mix the dry ingredients together, add them to the mixture and stir well to obtain a dough. Finally add the liqueur.

Carefully pour the dough into a greased and floured 2-litre cake tin and bake on the lower shelf of a 175°C oven for a good hour.

Turn the cake out of the tin and allow to cool under the tin.

Note:

You can make a suitable herbal sugar yourself, by mixing together 1 tsp dried mint, 2 tsp grated orange peel and 1 tsp ground fennel.

Banana Swiss roll

for the dough:

3 eggs

1 1/2 dl sugar

1/2 dl plain flour

1/2 dl potato flour

2 tbsp cocoa

1 tsp baking powder

for the filling:

2 dl thick cream

2 tbsp caster sugar

1 large banana, or two small ones

Heat the oven to 225°C. Line an oven tray with greaseproof paper.

Mix the flour, potato flour, cocoa and baking powder together. Beat the eggs and sugar into a froth and sieve the flour mixture into this. Stir thoroughly. Pour the dough onto the greaseproof paper and spread it to an even layer. Bake for about 5–6 minutes.

Sprinkle a thin layer of sugar on a new piece of paper. Turn the cake out onto the paper. Remove the original paper and allow the cake to cool.

Whip the cream and flavour with sugar. Mash the bananas to a coarse pulp with a fork. Spread first the banana pulp and then the whipped cream on the cake.

Form the cake into a roll with the help of the paper and tie it up. Place it in the fridge for a couple of hours to allow the filling to soak into the cake.

Serve cut into slices, or whole decorated with whipped cream and grated chocolate.

Cheese and berry flan *(marjatorttu)* made without an oven

for the flan case:

150 g oat or wholemeal biscuits

100 g melted butter

for the filling:

2 dl crème fraîche

or 200 g Philadelphia cream cheese

or the equivalent

2 egg yolks

1 dl sugar

1 dl fermented cream (kermaviili)

1 tsp vanilla sugar

2 egg whites

2 dl whipping cream

6 leaves of gelatine

1 dl pure orange or apple juice

for the topping:

1/2–1 litre strawberries, raspberries,

red or blackcurrants or cloudberries

some leaves of mint

Crush and grind the biscuits. Melt the butter and mix it in with them. Select a flan tin with a removable base. Cut a circle of greaseproof paper the size of its base and place it in the bottom of the tin. Press the biscuit crumb mixture into the bottom of the flan tin and place in the fridge while making the filling.

Soak the leaves of gelatine in plenty of cold water for about 10 minutes. Heat the orange or apple juice, squeeze most of the water out of the gelatine leaves and dissolve them in the hot juice. Do not cook.

Beat the egg yolks and sugar to a foam, and whisk the egg whites and the cream, both separately. Mix the crème fraîche or cream cheese and the fermented cream into the egg yolk mixture, add the gelatine mixture and stir well. Fold in the whipped cream and egg whites and flavour with vanilla sugar. When the mixture has nearly set, pour it onto the flan base.

Allow to set in the refrigerator. Cover the surface with berries and garnish with leaves of mint. Serve preferably the following day. Release from the flan tin by running a sharp knife around the inside edge.

Oatmeal biscuits *(kauralastut)*

(TO MAKE ABOUT 30 BISCUITS)

50 g melted butter or margarine

2 dl rolled porridge oats

1 1/2 dl sugar

1 tbsp plain flour

1 tsp baking powder

1 egg

Melt the butter or margarine and cool slightly. Combine the oats, sugar, flour, and baking powder, add the melted fat and stir. Beat the egg slightly and add to the batter.

Drop teaspoonfuls of batter onto an oven tray covered with greaseproof paper. Leave plenty of space between the biscuits, as they spread while cooking. Bake for about 6 minutes at 225°C.

Let the biscuits cool slightly before taking them off the paper, and make sure they are completely hard before stacking them in a biscuit tin.

Potato pasties
(vatruskat)

for the dough:

1 kg floury potatoes

1 1/2 dl plain flour

1/2–1 tbsp salt

2 eggs

for the filling:

cooked rice

chopped fried mushrooms

butter

Peel the potatoes and boil them in salted water. Mash them and add flour, eggs and salt. Form the dough into little balls and flatten them into round pasties about 10 cm in diameter with your floured hands.

Add some melted butter and the fried mushrooms to the rice and put a little of the filling into the centre of each pasty. Fold the pasties over into semi-circles. Press the edges together and put on a baking tray.

Prick the pasties with a fork. Bake at 250°C for about 10 minutes until golden brown. Brush with melted butter.

Salmon and rice pasty
(lohipiirakka)

for the pastry:

3 dl flour

200 g butter or margarine

about 1 dl cold water

or use ready-made puff pastry

for the filling:

3 dl cooked rice

2 hard-boiled eggs

a bunch of fresh dill

1 can of salmon

or 300 g fresh or slightly salted salmon

salt, white or black pepper

To make the pastry, cut the butter or margarine into the flour with two knives, a pastry blender, or your fingertips. When the mixture is granular, add the water and toss quickly to a dough. Let this dough stand in a cold place for a while.

Roll out the dough into a rectangular sheet about 1 cm thick on a floured baking table. Place half of the rice in the centre of the sheet, then add layers of sliced egg, salmon, chopped dill, seasonings and the rest of the rice.

Lift the edges of the pastry over the filling and press them together either with a fork or with your fingers. Brush the pastry with beaten egg and prick with a fork.

Bake in a 225°C oven until a golden brown, about 30 minutes.

Serve warm on its own or with melted butter seasoned with dill.

Quark tart
(rahkapiirakka)

for the dough:

75 g soft butter

1/2 dl sugar

1 egg

30 g fresh yeast, or 11 g dried yeast

2 dl milk

1 tsp salt

6 dl plain flour

for the filling:

250 g quark or cream cheese

1 dl sugar

1 dl cream

1 egg

1/2 dl raisins

1/2 tsp vanillin

1–2 tbsp lemon juice

Cream the butter and sugar, add the egg and beat well. Dissolve the yeast in the lukewarm milk and add this liquid and the salt to the butter mixture. Add the flour gradually, knead well and allow to rise.

Turn the dough out onto a piece of greaseproof paper on an oven tray and roll to a sheet about 1 cm thick. Allow to rise again.

Combine all of the ingredients for the filling and stir until smooth.

Spread the filling evenly over the crust and bake at 200°C for about 30 minutes.

Round individual quark tarts

Divide the dough into 12–16 parts. Shape each into a round bun and put on an oven tray to rise. Press each down in the centre with a flat-bottomed drinking class to form a tart shape and fill the hollow with the quark mixture. Brush the edges with egg and bake at 225°C for 15 minutes.

A quick and easy fruit pie

1 egg

1 dl sugar

100 g butter or margarine, melted

3 dl plain flour

1 tsp baking powder

(1 tsp vanilla sugar)

for the filling:

1/2–1 litre bilberries, pieces of rhubarb or slices of apple

1/2–1 dl granulated or brown sugar

Melt and cool the butter. Whip the egg and sugar to a froth and add the cooled melted butter.

Mix the flour, baking powder and vanilla sugar together and fold into the whipped egg mixture.

Put about a quarter of the dough on one side and spread the rest on the bottom of a round pie tin and a little up the sides. Fill with the fruit and sprinkle the granulated or brown sugar on the top of it. Decorate the top with knobs of the dough that was put on one side.

Bake on the bottom shelf of a 200°C oven for about half an hour.

The Land of Healthy Bread

The most popular modern forms of bread are portion-sized pieces of white bread, granary bread or rye bread that are sold ready sliced in half.

The power of bread lies in its origins. When you hold a loaf of bread in your hand and cut suitably-sized slices off it you come into direct contact with the grain field, with nature and growth. Anyone who is interested in the whole culture surrounding bread can make new discoveries equally well by examining industrially produced bread as by going into the selections offered by small, traditional bakers, rural outlets, market places and market halls.

The basic ingredients of Finnish bread are rye, oats and barley, and it is not uncommon to combine all of these grains. The health-promoting effects of the fibres in natural grains have been demonstrated scientifically, particularly in the case of rye and oats, and one outcome of this has been the development of a fibre concentrate which can be used to enrich both white and brown bread. The beneficial effects of rye on coronary functions are undeniable, while oats has been shown to reduce blood cholesterol.

Although plain white bread baked from wheat flour is gaining ground, our bread baskets still have room for local varieties, and pure wheat bread is in a way considered so "fine" that it is usually referred to as "French bread". The most popular bread of all at the present moment is made of a mixture of grains.

In olden times the country was split in two as regards bread baking customs. It was common in the west to bake bread only occasionally and to eat hard, dry bread, while people in the east would light their baking ovens once a week, normally at weekends, and make fresh bread and pasties. It is difficult to draw a line between these two areas nowadays, but the basic traditions live on. A hole in the centre of a loaf is a reminder of the days when they were hung up on

Twelve good reasons for eating rye bread:

1. It smells and tastes so good.
2. It helps you to control your weight.
3. It gives you a well-fed feeling.
4. It gives you stamina.
5. It keeps your blood sugar steady.
6. It keeps your teeth and gums in trim.
7. It improves your digestion.
8. It helps to lower cholesterol levels.
9. It can prevent the development of type 2 diabetes.
10. It purges and nurtures the intestines.
11. It protects the heart.
12. It reduces the risk of cancer.

a rail to dry. The resulting dry ring loaves can be thought of as the ancestors of our crispbreads and rye rusks.

The shapes of the loaves are also traditional, being circular and rounded on the top in the east of the country and flat, often unleavened, in the north.

Rye bread

The rye loaf baked from a sour, leavened dough is one of the icons of the world of Finnish food. It has been voted the Finns' favourite food on numerous occasions and is also known to be one of the best sources of fibre. Some small bakeries and private homes may well have leaven in their bowl that has been kept alive for more than a hundred years. The art of making this bread originally spread to Finland from the east and reached every corner of the country. The most recent industrial products such as ready-split rye sandwich bread, rye rolls and the like, which are easy to use and very popular, have been developed from this same rye dough, and their special soured quality is still governed by the same preferences in terms of taste.

Sometimes other aesthetic qualities are detected in bread, too, as it has been said of one industrially produced oval-shaped rye bread roll that "It is a prime example of the benefits of design." It is true that these rolls look interesting and attractive as well as smelling divine and feeling fresh and pleasant to the touch

Rieska and rievä

These are two words used for local types of bread, each varying greatly in meaning from one region to another. *Rieska*, for instance, can be either a

Oat rolls
(kaurasämpylät)

2 1/2 dl milk
1 tsp salt
2 tbsp treacle
25 g fresh yeast,
or 11 g of dried yeast
2 tsp ground anise
4 dl rolled porridge oats (quick-cooking)
4 1/2 dl plain flour
50 g butter

Dissolve the yeast in warm milk and add the salt, sugar and anise. Mix in the oats, flour and finally the butter. Let the dough rise until doubled in size. Form into rolls. Let them rise again and bake at 225°C for 5–8 minutes. Serve immediately while still warm, or heat again later.

Rolls and bread baked from whole-grain flour are taken for granted nowadays.

Whole-wheat rolls *(grahamsämpylät)*

2 1/2 dl milk
25 g fresh yeast,
or 11 g of dried yeast
1 1/2 tsp salt
1/2 dl treacle
2 dl plain flour
3 1/2 dl whole-wheat (graham) flour
50 g butter

Dissolve the yeast in the lukewarm milk and add the salt and treacle. Mix in the flour and finally the softened butter and knead to a smooth dough. Let the dough rise. Form into rolls and let these rise again. Bake at 225°C for 10–12 minutes.

round-topped loaf of yeast bread or a flat slab of unleavened bread, while *rievä*, as used in Häme, means a tasty white bread based on a yeast dough made from barley flour. The most famous variety of this comes from Tampere, where it is sold in paper bags with a waltz tune dedicated to it printed on the outside. This has even found its way into the Guinness Book of Records as "the world's most widely published sheet music".

Sweet varieties of bread

Sweet spiced breads made with soured milk and potatoes are popular on the coast and in the west of Finland. The "island bread", containing malt and syrup, is especially good with Baltic herrings or

other forms of fish, and the flat black bread of Åland is still sweeter.

At Christmas everything is sweet, and a sweetish Christmas bread made with soured milk, spiced with anis and fennel and brushed on the top with a mixture of water and syrup is common throughout the country.

Crispbreads

Crispbread, *näkkileipä*, and crisp rye bread, *hapankorppu*, are everyday purchases for Finnish households. Crispbreads are good for the teeth and are a useful standby for home and school, and for the army, which is said to march on the strength of its crispbread. Rusks are lighter and have a number of culinary uses.

A very thin variety of rye or barley crispbread, rather like a biscuit, has been produced for centuries at small bakeries in Finland, especially those on the landed estates, and this has been revived in recent times as a gourmet product. Crispbread is now a popular export item that is sold in around fifty countries.

Novel forms of bread

The bread market in Finland is flourishing at the moment. White French loaves, ciabatta, olive bread, bread containing raisins or various seeds, and carrot bread are all to be found in the supermarkets and bakeries, in addition to the more prosaic white breads and barley breads. Bread is something to be enjoyed, and increasing attention is being paid to its quality, and above all to its healthiness. The majority of shoppers prefer wholemeal bread, and the selection of toast bread has improved with the introduction of rye bread for toasting.

This nation of coffee-drinkers is also fond of tea. The thin crispbread pictured here is exported to as many as 50 countries.

Potato bread *(perunarieskat)*

1/2 litre mashed potato
1 tsp salt
1 egg
about 2 1/2 dl barley flour

Add the salt, egg and barley flour to the mashed potato to make a dough, which should not be too soft. Divide the dough in two. Flour your hands well and pat the dough into two flat loaves on an oven tray covered with greaseproof paper. The loaves should be 1/2–1 cm thick. You can also make several small loaves about 10 cm in diameter.
Bake at 275°C for 15–25 minutes. Serve hot with butter.

Finnish Meat and Poultry

The meat produced in Finland is of exceptionally high quality and has survived the various scandals that have hit the world meat market with a clean bill of health.

There are not many traditional butchers' shops left, but it is possible to go through the selection of meat products available fairly well on the basis of market stalls and the meat counters of supermarkets. More and more meat is being sold ready packed, and the market is undoubtedly dominated by pork, although chicken is catching up fast to become a basic ingredient for Finnish cuisine. Convenience is all-important in our day and age, so that strips of chicken, flavoured or marinaded in various ways, have become the "minced meat of the 21st century". There is also an increased interest in turkey and goose meat.

Minced meat as such is a firm favourite, of course, because of the status of meat balls, minced meat sauce and minced meat and macaroni baked in the oven as the much-loved staple foods of most Finns. Many other former favourites have nevertheless been ousted in recent times by the introduction of new methods of preparation and stronger seasonings. Fatty pork in gravy is one old-time dish that many elderly people crave for, and most butchers at market stalls, for instance, will know what is meant by "gravy meat" – boneless belly of pork for crisp-frying to make *tirripaisti* or for adding to *kalakukko*. The height of the season for pork is nevertheless Christmas, when the centrepiece of the dinner table for most households is the Christmas ham.

The third most popular meat is beef, which is used mainly for steaks and roast joints, although a

Finnish lamb is a particularly tasty meat.

great deal is also sold nowadays cut into strips or into pieces suitable for a wok.

Roast lamb is mostly a festive dish for Easter, but lamb meat are eaten more generally at other times of the year. Lamb can also be combined with cabbage to make either a stew or a soup, or else a minced lamb casserole in the oven or cabbage rolls in which a cabbage leaf is wrapped round a core of minced lamb.

Lamb is also excellent smoked. A whole leg of smoked lamb is known as a "violin" (*lampaanviulu*), while *rosvopaisti* (robbers' roast) is a ritual meal that can be tried with guests some time. The idea comes from the novel *Lampaansyöjät* (The Sheep Eaters) by Veikko Huovinen, in which two white-collar workers who have set out on a drinking spree steal a sheep and cook it in a pit dug in the ground.

Vorschmack is a dish made and popularized by Field-Marshal Carl Gustav Mannerheim, a notable gourmet for whom this was his favourite food. It consists of herring and minced cooked lamb, usually the scraps left over from a joint of roast lamb. The two are mixed together and baked slowly in the oven. It is a lunchtime speciality in a number of restaurants in Helsinki, most notably the Savoy. It is served with smetana and a mixture of chopped pickled cucumber and pickled beetroot.

Livestock rearing has for a long time been an important aspect of farming in Finland, and this has become more diversified recently, so that farms may now have buffaloes and wild boar grazing in their fields as well as pigs and beef cattle. There are relatively few sheep left, however; only about 80,000 ewes over the whole country. They are most visible in the landscape of Åland and Northern Finland. The latest arrivals are ostriches, emus, ducks and geese, all of which are raised on farms to some extent.

The original Karelian stew can be supplemented with onions and root vegetables if you wish.

Karelian stew *(karjalanpaisti)*

1/2 kg boned beef
1/4 kg boned lamb
1/4 kg boned pork
1 veal kidney
250 g liver
(1 onion)
(1–2 carrots)
8 whole allspice
1 tbsp salt
water

Trim the meats and cut into 3 x 3 cm cubes. Peel the onions and carrots and cut them into pieces. Place these in layers with the spices in an ovenproof casserole, with the pork on the top.

Add enough water to cover.

Cook without a lid in a hot oven (225°C) at first, to brown the meat, and then cover and reduce the temperature to 175°C. Cook for 2–3 hours altogether.

Meatballs
(lihapullat)

500 g minced meat (2/3 beef, 1/3 pork)
1 dl dry breadcrumbs
2 dl water, or water and cream
1 small onion
1 1/2 tsp salt
white pepper
(thyme, garlic)
1 egg
butter, margarine, or oil for frying

Soak the breadcrumbs in the liquid to swell them. Finely chop the onion and lightly fry the pieces in butter. Cool.

Mix all the ingredients together in a bowl and season with salt and pepper, adding other seasonings if you like.

Mould the meat into balls with your wet hands and fry them in fat until a golden brown and done all the way through.

Serve hot or cold.

Mashed potatoes

1 kg floury potatoes
water, salt
2 tbsp butter
2 dl milk
(1 tsp sugar)
2 tsp salt

Peel the potatoes and boil in a small amount of salted water until soft.

Pour off the water, mash the potatoes and add butter, salt (sugar) and hot milk. Whisk until fluffy. Serve immediately.

Vorschmack

1/2 kg roast lamb
1 salted herring fillet, soaked,
or matjes herring fillet
2 onions, diced
butter
juices from the roast, or meat stock
1/2–1 tbsp mustard
white pepper
1 dl cream
6 Scandinavian-style anchovy fillets

To be served with:
sour cream
diced pickled cucumbers
diced pickled beetroot

Clean and fillet the herring. Cut the roast lamb into pieces. Put the lamb and herring through a meat mincer or chop coarsely in a food processor.

Melt the butter in a thick-bottomed pot. Fry the onions until they are a golden brown. Add the minced meat mixture.

Add just enough stock or juice from the roasting of the lamb to give it a porridge-like consistency. Bring the mixture to the boil. Season and add cream.

Simmer for 1/2–1 hour, or even longer, stirring from time to time. Be careful that it does not stick.

Put the mixture in an oven-proof dish and bake for 45 minutes at 175°C.

Serve in the dish, with pickled cucumber, beetroot and sour cream put out separately.

You can also use vorschmack as a filling for crêpes or omelettes.

The soft Finnish meat balls are a favourite with children and adults alike.

Reindeer meat for the connoisseur

The "cattle of Lapland" are the herds of the semi-domesticated reindeer, *Rangifer tarandus*, a distant relative of the American caribou. The herding of reindeer is largely in the hands of the original inhabitants and constitutes one of the major sources of livelihood in the north, where a total of about 300,000 reindeer share a "giant grazing ground" that accounts for 36% of the surface area of Finland. Although the reindeer roam wild in the countryside, they are not hunted but are rounded up between October and February or March each year and slaughtered by their owners as required. The meat is fine-grained and low in fat, comparable to the best game that can be had. One has to be careful when ordering or buying reindeer meat, however, as ordinary venison, which tastes very much the same, is sometimes sold under the same name. Frozen reindeer meat is available throughout the year in all parts of the country.

Although dark in colour, reindeer meat is surprisingly mild to the taste, and in spite of its low fat content it is rich in valuable nutrients and easily digested. The secret of its flavour lies in the diet of the reindeer themselves, first of all the mother's milk, followed by leaves, grass, wild mushrooms and the lichens that are common in the northern forests.

Reindeer can be used in more or less all kinds of meat dishes, and does not necessarily call for any special garnishes. Suitable accompaniments are onions, carrots, celery, parsnip or pickled cucumber, while the natural products that go particularly well with it include mushrooms and berries, crushed lingonberries, cranberries or

The reindeer are the cattle of Lapland. They are slaughtered in autumn and winter.

Flakes of reindeer meat for stewing are pared off a lump of frozen meat with a sharp knife.

Reindeer stew *(poronkäristys)*

1 kg boneless, frozen reindeer meat (rump or shoulder)
100–200 g lard or butter
water
salt
(white pepper, onions)

Cut the lard or butter into very small cubes and heat in a cast-iron pot or casserole.

Cut the meat into flakes while still frozen. You can also buy reindeer meat prepared in this way. Add the frozen meat to the pot. Cover and simmer.

When all the water from the frozen meat has evaporated, the clear liquid remaining will be the fat in which the meat will brown. Add a little more water and continue simmering for half an hour or more, until the meat is tender. You can add chopped onions and white pepper at this stage, if you like. Add salt to taste.

Serve with mashed potatoes seasoned with finely chopped onions cooked slowly in butter.

rowanberries or the equivalent jams. Some dishes will also benefit from a dash of cream.

Reindeer liver and reindeer heart are more specialized products, while a cold-smoked joint of reindeer will provide excellent cold meat for sandwiches as well as being a delicious main course.

Flakes of salty reindeer meat dried in the open air make a good aperitif, and they are particularly tasty when heated over an open fire until they are crisp. Dried meat has traditionally been a staple food for the people of Lapland to take with them on journeys.

There is at least one reindeer dish that is among the essential things to experience in Lapland, and that is reindeer stew, *poronkäristys*, which is at its best when ladled out straight from the sooty black pot in which it has been cooked over a campfire.

The recipe is an ancient and very simple one, and is the same regardless of whether the dish is made at home or on the fells. Thin flakes are whittled off a frozen lump of meat with a sheath-knife and fried rapidly in reindeer fat, lard or butter in a hot frying pan or in the bottom of the cooking pot. They are then seasoned with salt and either water or snow is added, and the stew is boiled for a suitable length of time. It is eaten with buttery mashed potatoes and lingonberries.

It is possible to buy reindeer meat even in the south of Finland. A half of all the meat is sold frozen, and fresh meat, sausages, prepared dishes and canned meat are also obtainable. One popular form is the dark-coloured smoked reindeer meat, which keeps especially well and makes good cold slices for eating on bread or in salads. Frozen reindeer meat is suitable for soups and stews and for making a delicious reindeer pie.

Game and wildfowl

Although the number of game animals is limited by the barren natural environment and the severe winters, the selection of meat available to a household is filled out by the various forms of game that happen to be in season. Finland has over 300,000 registered hunters, of whom about 14,000 are women. All hunters are required to pass an examination.

The outstanding large game animal is the elk, or moose, the Lord of the Forest. It is even possible occasionally to see a stray elk early in the morning in the streets of Helsinki, and drivers should be on the look-out for elk running onto the roads at almost any time. Teams of elk hunters with their red woolly hats and red vests are a common sight in the forests in autumn. Some hunting clubs arrange elk hunts in which fee-paying outsiders can take part.

Elk find their food in the forests, eating mostly grass, dwarf shrubs, twigs and the buds of trees and bushes. As a result, their meat has a genuine gamey flavour and is low in fat and rich in protein. They can be hunted from the last Saturday in September until the middle of December, and the numbers that can be culled in a given area are laid down by the game conservation authorities.

Other forms of deer that are hunted in Finland are the *white-tailed deer, wild forest reindeer* and *fallow deer,* and also the *roe deer,* the population of which has increased in recent times, so that it is likely to be an important game animal in the future.

Wild boar spread into Finland from the Soviet Union, and are nowadays raised in captivity, so that some of those living in the wild belong to the original wild population and some are feralized animals that have escaped from farms. Even in captivity the wild boar live out of doors all the year round and behave

The Finns' own big game animal is the elk.

Willow grouse in a creamy game sauce

2 young oven-ready willow grouse
2 tsp salt
a pinch of white pepper
for cooking:
butter
3–4 dl stock or water
for the sauce:
2 1/2 dl juice from cooking the grouse
2 1/2 tbsp plain flour
2 dl cream
salt
1–2 tsp blackcurrant jelly
(1–2 tsp blue cheese)

Clean the birds and brown them well in butter in a casserole with a lid. Sprinkle with salt and white pepper.

Add stock, cover and simmer for approximately 45 minutes until the birds are well done.

Pour the juice from cooking through a sieve into a small pan. Mix the flour with some cold water and whisk it into the juice. Boil for about 5 minutes. Add cream and seasoning. Simmer for a couple of minutes. Bone the grouse and arrange the pieces of meat on a serving dish. Pour the hot sauce over the meat. Puréed lingonberries are a traditional side dish, while jams made from other berries and raw vegetable salads are newer forms of accompaniment.

A willow grouse in its winter plumage.

in their accustomed manner. Wild boars take three times longer to grow to a commercially exploitable size than do domestic pigs and their meat is denser than pork, darker and with a distinct gamey taste. Those living in the wild are hunted as game.

Although *bear* meat dishes are served in some restaurants, bears are a protected species and special permission is required for hunting them.

The *blue hare* and *brown hare* thrive all over the country, and their meat is eaten regularly in hunting families and is a speciality of some restaurants. Finnish hare meat is not available in shops, however.

The main wildfowl shot in Finland are *mallard duck*, *capercaillie*, *black grouse*, *hazel hen* and *willow grouse*, of which mallard duck and willow grouse can be sold in shops. The willow grouse is the northernmost of the Finnish wildfowl species, inhabiting the fells of Lapland, where it exchanges its brownish plumage for white in the winter. It lives off a diet of seeds and berries, and also birch buds in winter, and its meat is dark, fine-grained and tasty. It is traditionally either trapped or shot.

Willow grouse, potatoes, cream sauce and berry jelly.

Elk meat can be prepared in many ways: this minced meat steak is served with lingonberry butter.

Minced elk meat steaks with lingonberry butter

1/2 kg boneless elk meat or venison
5 dl whipping cream
about 1 tbsp salt (13 g)
1/2 tsp ground black pepper from a mill
1 egg

Cut the meat into cubes. Have all the other ingredients at the ready. Make sure that they are all cold before you begin mincing the meat.

Put the cubes of meat into a multimixer and mince them well. Add the cream in a stream as the machine is running, and then add the salt and finally the egg. Be careful not to mince the meat for too long, or it may turn liquid. Press the minced meat through a sieve and put it on one side in the cold.

Form the meat into cakes with your damp hands and fry them in a pan. Alternatively, you can form the cakes in metal rings and cook them on a tray in the oven. Allow to cool.

Re-heat the steaks in butter in a frying pan just before serving, giving them a beautiful golden colour.

Lingonberry butter

250 g butter
1/2 dl smooth, sharp lingonberry purée
1 clove of garlic
a sprig of rosemary, finely chopped
salt and black pepper

Heat the lingonberry purée and add the pressed garlic, rosemary, pepper and salt. Bring to the boil, sieve and cool.

Beat the butter to a froth in a liquidizer and add the purée, beating well. Roll the lingonberry butter into sticks between pieces of cling foil. Freeze, and slice onto steaks as required.

Red wine sauce

3 shallots, cut into small cubes
3 cloves of garlic, split in two lengthways
3 tbsp butter
a bay leaf
salt
a small bunch of thyme
5 whole white peppers
2 tbsp red wine vinegar
1 dl red port wine
4 dl red wine
5 dl meat stock

Heat the shallots, garlic, herbs, seasoning and butter in a saucepan and fry them lightly for about 5 minutes. Add the vinegar and boil it off. Then add the wine and reduce the stock to about a decilitre.

Pour in the meat stock and reduce to about half of the original volume. Sieve the sauce and check for taste.

Roast wild duck with apples and a creamy game sauce

2 wild ducks (weighing 500–800 g each)

butter

salt and white pepper

for the roasting dish:

4 beetroots

10 young beetroots with tops

4 carrots

50 g butter

a sprig of rosemary

salt and black pepper

Peel and dice the vegetables and spread them on a deep oven tray. Season with salt and pepper and rosemary leaves.

Fry the ducks in butter in a frying pan until they are browned all over. Rub salt and white pepper into the surfaces and place them on top of the vegetables on the oven tray.

Cook them in the oven for about 40 minutes at 125°C. They will be done when their inside temperature is above 60°C. Cover them in aluminium foil and allow to stand for 1/2 hour before carving.

Apples in sugared butter

8 segments of firm-textured apples

1/2 tbsp butter

2 tsp sugar

a pinch of salt

Heat the butter in a broad, shallow saucepan and place the apple segments side by side on the bottom. Sprinkle sugar on them and fry them, turning them over to make sure that they gain a colour on all sides. Season with salt if necessary. Check that they are properly cooked.

Creamy game sauce

for the stock:

1 litre good duck stock

a piece of celeriac

a piece of parsnip

1 carrot

1 onion

2 tbsp butter

a sprig of rosemary

a small bunch of thyme

1/2 tsp whole seeds of allspice

2 tbsp cognac

for the sauce:

1/2 litre concentrated stock

2 tbsp blue cheese (Finnish Aura cheese)

2 tbsp blackcurrant jelly

salt and black pepper from a mill

2 dl whipped cream

Peel and dice the vegetables, including the onion, and fry them lightly with the herbs in the bottom of a saucepan until they are partially cooked. Add the cognac and duck stock.

Allow them to boil gently for 30 minutes, and then sieve. Reduce the stock to about half a litre and flavour with Aura cheese and blackcurrant jelly. Sieve again if necessary.

Check for taste and add the whipped cream to the sauce before serving.

Old-time roast wild mallard duck with cream sauce.

The Land of Sausages

"Sauna sausage" with mustard is a familiar, much loved everyday meal, or something to eat after sauna or on an outing in the country.

Finland is a land of sausages, *makkara*, even though not everybody would be prepared to admit it. They serve both as a food to take on trips to the countryside and as a delicacy to be enjoyed at home. Whole market days can be held on the theme of sausages. Almost all the cooked sausages and salamis are available in light, low-fat versions, and "lighter than light" now seems to be the order of the day.

The pride of place among Finnish sausages belongs to the "sauna sausage", or *lenkkimakkara*, which is especially popular for grilling out of doors in summer. The most famous make of this is the "HK Blue" which is commemorated annually on its own "feast-day".

Sausages are equally tasty hot or cold. The Finnish rally drivers have taught their colleagues to grill sausages over a campfire during their breaks in the same way as they would in the forest at home in Finland. *Lenkkimakkara* cooked in the oven is a popular luncheon dish at schools and in works' canteens, and the smell of it being grilled or cooked on an open fire is an essentially part of a sauna evening.

Sausage eaters all have their own preferences and rituals. Children and those who are up and about at night tend to prefer small Frankfurters, *nakki*, while those who queue at street corner grills tend to go for hot dogs and various sausage concoctions such as the "Pori burger", a thick lump of garlic sausage between two slices of toast, the "Turku burger" which uses bacon sausage for the same purpose, or the "Hydrogen and Atom" to be found in both Lappeenranta and Pori, which is a deep-fried meat pie filled with a boiled egg and boiled or smoked ham.

Common sausage dishes:

Sausage cooked in the oven, sausage soup, sausage sauce, sausage Stroganoff, *siskonmakkara* soup, *siskonmakkara* stew, sausage pizza, sausage pasta, sausage *(nakki)* and mash, and even Caesar salad with sausage.

When the person behind the counter asks whether you want your sausage, "with all the trimmings", this will mean mustard, ketchup, chopped onions and garlic, cucumber relish and the like. What would the President of Finland choose when popping out to the street-corner grill after an evening of celebrating an election victory?

The true companion of Finnish sausage is smooth, sweet mustard, either mild or hot, although small firms bring new flavours onto the market practically every year: garlic, cognac, herbs, chilli, sal ammoniac, *pontikka* or tar mustard.

Small *nakki* sausages eaten with cold potato salad are a must for some people at the New Year and on May Day, for instance, while others prefer their

Black pudding needs lingonberries to go with it, in either a jam or a sauce.

sausages raw or yearn nostalgically for thick slices of pale Bologna sausage, *lauantaimakkara*, which can be piled onto pieces of plain white bread in moments of extreme homesickness.

The art of making sausages at home has not disappeared; on the contrary, it is going through a revival at the moment. Devotees of sausage will meet together to make and eat home-made sausages, and new, tasty varieties are constantly being developed by both large and small meat processing companies. The new flavours on the market are frequently exotic or hot, but the basic recipes behind them are often the traditional ones. Sausages are usually made of pork or beef, but you can also find lamb, elk, reindeer, wild boar, goose and ostrich sausages, and gourmet restaurants have been known to serve sweetbread sausages and salmon sausages, or other unusual specialities such as cheese, mushroom or vegetable sausages. When a Finn comes up against the Irish blood sausage, his thoughts immediately return to Tampere, the home of the Finnish black sausage, as it is called, which is filled out with pearl barley or rye grains, giving you more to chew on. There are also conventional meat sausages with these grains added, which attract a clientele of their own.

Our oldest commercially made type of sausage is a pale pork sausage known as *siskonmakkara*, while other fresh sausages, which have to be cooked before eating, are the Lakenwurst, *laukkamakkara*, and raisin sausage produced in Southwestern Finland. There are also places where raw potatoes are put into sausages.

Finnish connoisseurs of sausage are naturally also familiar with chorizo and bratwurst, and are accustomed to washing their sausage down with the only possible drink, beer.

Cheeses for All Occasions

Cheese has become a trendy food nowadays, and the Finns' consumption of cheese has doubled over the last fifty years, reflecting the accent on health, ease of preparation, quickness and enjoyment in eating. Stronger, matured low-fat cheeses in particular have found their way onto the nation's slices of bread, while the selection of unripened cheeses has increased greatly and ready-sliced cheeses, grated cheeses and individually wrapped portions of cheese spread have come onto the market to make it easier to serve cheese than ever before.

Although the Cheese Society has tried to teach people to cut their cheese into thick chunks, the traditional cheese slicer is still an essential implement in most homes. Edam is the favourite everyday cheese for the average Finn, but a selection of cheeses will readily be brought out for supper amongst the family or when entertaining friends.

Cheese has been produced industrially in Finland for some 150 years, the skills for this having been brought from Switzerland, as was one

Finland has a fine blue cheese of its very own.

Emmenthal cheese is a much sought-after Finnish export product.

Piimä or egg cheese is made of cow's milk, eggs and the soured milk product *piimä*.

of the most familiar types of cheese, Emmenthal, of which several varieties differing in age are produced in this country. The degree of maturity of an Emmenthal cheese is stamped on the rind and shown on the packet: blue, red or black label.

Low-fat (15–17%) and low-salt cheeses have gained in popularity, and the tasty low-fat *Polar 5* cheese, where the 5 refers to the percentage of fat, has become a major export item. *Turunmaa* is a grainy, aerated cheese that has been developed entirely in Finland. Cheese spreads are used not only on bread but also for thickening sauces and soups.

The traditional Finnish cheeses include goat's cheese, soured milk or egg cheese and the brown-spotted "bread cheese", *leipäjuusto*, Ostrobothnia's gift to the rest of Finland. This latter was originally made in the form of a disc and was cooked in front of the fire. It is especially delicious when warmed up with cream and served with cloudberry jam. All these cheeses belong to the traditional buffet tables of their regions and are best when made at home by skilled housewives.

The Finns appear to have fallen in love with blue cheese, which they even use to garnish smoked reindeer pizza! The Finnish *Aura* cheese is a favourite, especially on ginger biscuits.

Many small family diaries have emerged recently that have developed new, tasty cheeses made from cow's or goat's milk and flavored with boldky selected new ingredients, including herbs. Thus, although there is an enormous selection of cheeses available today, both Finnish and foreign, it is quite possible to put together an impressive cheeseboard of both hard and soft varieties entirely from cheeses produced in Finland.

Home-made cheese *(piimäjuusto)*

3 litres milk
1 litre buttermilk (piimä)
3 eggs
salt

Whisk the buttermilk and eggs. Heat the milk and add the buttermilk and egg mixture to it when it boils, beating well. Turn off the stove, but let the saucepan stay on the hotplate until the cheese settles. Line a cheese mould or a sieve with a cheese cloth and ladle the cheese in with a slotted spoon. Sprinkle salt between the layers. Cover the mould or sieve with a plate or other weight. Store in a cold place and serve the following day.

What Will You Have to Drink?

Milk, and alongside it the soured milk known as *piimä*, are the customary drinks at everyday family meals and serve as an important daily source of protein, calcium and vitamins. Although the consumption of milk has decreased somewhat with the greater interest in water, fruit juices and soft drinks, fat-free milk has become very much more popular, so that it now accounts for 30% of all sales of milk. The most widely drunk variety of milk is nevertheless that known as "light milk", with a fat content of 2.5%. *Piimä* has always been an excellent, healthy drink, and it has now become common to enrich it with various lactobacilli that are good for the digestion, improve resistance to infection and settle the stomach.

Although the thirst-quenching juices that used to be made at home from wild or cultivated berries have been largely replaced by international-style soft drinks, a number of small breweries and soft drinks companies have been trying to revive the old recipes and produce fizzy lemonades on the basis of them. It is the custom at the President's summer residence of Kultaranta in Naantali to serve rhubarb juice as an aperitif in June, followed by currant juice once the currants have ripened. These juices are still made in the traditional way, by steaming in a large double saucepan, as is done in most homes. Blackcurrant juice is also a popular remedy for 'flu in winter.

The mead drink *sima* could easily have become the national beverage, but it has never really been "discovered" commercially yet and has remained very much a seasonal product, which is – unfortunately – only made once a year even by the largest soft drinks companies. One good thing is that

Many people believe that the best thirst-quencher in summer is cold home-made juice made from wild or cultivated berries, and the same juice is excellent hot in winter.

Strawberry and yoghurt milkshake

(FOR 2 PERSONS)

2 dl strawberries
2 tsp sugar
2 dl milk
2 dl natural yoghurt

Measure the ingredients into a jug. Whip to a froth with a hand-held mixer and pour into tall glasses.

A healthy smoothie

(FOR 2 PERSONS)

10–15 strawberries
3 dl soured milk (piimä) or yoghurt
1/2 dl oat bran
2 tbsp sugar
a pinch of vanilla sugar

Measure the ingredients into a jug. Whip with a hand-held mixer until smooth.

Allow to cool in the fridge for 5 minutes before drinking.

a number of small firms have started bottling *sima* made according to their own recipes.

The Finns are demanding when it comes to water. The tap water and well water is good practically everywhere, but those who are accustomed to drinking spring water will not settle for anything less, and they will sometimes travel long distances with their canisters to collect it. Finland is already exporting bottled spring and well water to countries which suffer from a water shortage.

Before the days of milk the staple drink was a home-brewed beer, and this is still a popular non-alcoholic drink, especially in summer.

Beer, sahti and other stronger thirst-quenchers

The Finns have been brewing beer and distilling spirits for hundreds of years, and the attitude towards such matters is well summed up in the legendary comment by a man whose companion was proposing a toast: "Have we come here to talk or to drink?"

Beer is popular with meals and goes well with most traditional foods. The six-pack is a common sight in supermarket trolleys these days, or even the 12-bottle pack that has come to be known affectionately as a "Dachshund". Similarly the pub culture has spread throughout the country and women are also drinking beer, although most tend to prefer cider.

Although the beer market is dominated by a small number of giant firms, it is gratifying to see that many small breweries selling their products locally have appeared all over the country, some with pubs or restaurants of their own. The high quality of the spring water and groundwater is one of the secrets behind the success of Finnish beer. The Finns themselves tend to prefer lager beers of varying strengths both with meals and for quenching

Home-brewed beer

5 litres water
1/2 litre malt
3 dl sugar
1/2 tsp fresh yeast,
or a pinch of dried yeast
1 tbsp hops

Bring the water to the boil and pour it on top of the malt, sugar and hops in a large jug. Mix well. Cool the mixture until it is lukewarm. Add the yeast dissolved in a little of the liquid.
Keep at room temperature until the beer has clearly fermented. This will take about a day.
Sieve and bottle the beer. Store in a cool place. It will be ready to drink the next day.

the thirst, and practically alcohol-free beer is also produced commercially. Imported beers have nevertheless captured substantial lengths of shelf space in the shops, and the selection now includes beers from most parts of the world. Beer with an alcohol content of less than 4.5% can be sold in supermarkets and even at filling stations, but stronger varieties are confined to the outlets of the state alcohol monopoly Alko.

The routine after sauna is to cool off with a drink of beer, juice or lemonade, and then to cook some sausage and make a pot of sauna coffee.

Sahti is an unusual drink from the past, the "mother of all beers". It is a drink that used to be made at home just two or three days before a celebration, and when made in the traditional way it is a cloudy liquid that is light brown in colour if made mainly with barley or dark if made with rye and has an alcohol content of 7–8%. It is still made and drunk nowadays when a group of people gather to work together or at celebrations such as weddings and funerals. It is also good for drinking after sauna, to complete the experience as described by the beer guru Michael Jackson, "First you go to sauna, then you jump into the lake and then you have some *sahti* ... and the sun never sets at all."

There are a few firms that brew *sahti* commercially, and the products can be ordered through Alko or directly from the firms' own sales outlets. The places where the breweries are located have their own *sahti* bars and brewmasters. It is also possible to buy a wort from which you can brew your own *sahti* at home. Brewing competitions are organized every year, the participants being chosen on the strength of qualifying rounds.

Cider

Alcoholic ciders are the favourite drinks of women and young people. Most bars sell draught cider alongside draught beer, and the stronger ciders, both Finnish and imported are also sold in Alko shops, while those with a lower alcohol content are sold in ordinary food shops.

A long drink, "*lonkero*", is a term that covers various ready-mixed drinks based on vodka or gin, to which aromas of one kind or another have been added. The most common flavours are grapefruit and pineapple, and the latest newcomer is a fresh, sharp apple flavour.

Wines

The Finns appreciate good wines, and both the supply and consumption of wines have increased vastly in recent years. Both reasonably priced everyday wines and high quality wines are now available from most of the world's wine-producing countries.

Wine is drunk both for its own sake and as an accompaniment to food, usually at celebrations or at moments when a family can enjoy good food at the weekend, and much less often on an everyday basis.

This stylish set of glasses is of Finnish design.

The tasting and collecting of wines can be a fascinating hobby, and this has given rise to wine clubs in most parts of the country. Some of these have constructed pleasant meeting places with their own cellars and wine tasting facilities in the basements of old houses.

Local wineries

Although small-scale commercial wine making is a relatively new venture in Finland, having begun only in 1995, there are now about 50 wineries that are licensed to produce alcoholic beverages from local fruits and berries. The wines are normally bought direct from the producers, but liqueurs and distilled products, which can often be tasted at the wineries, can be purchased only through Alko.

Most of the raw materials used in the production of berry liqueurs come from the forests and mires, or else are supplied by commercial strawberry, raspberry, bilberry or sea buckthorn growers. The conditions of the operating licence stipulate that 50% of the raw materials used in the making of local wines must be grown at the winery or under contract from it. These wineries have in many cases become places for the whole family to visit, with opportunities to taste the wines, have a meal, go fishing and walk round nature trails, etc.

A Calvados-type fortified wine is produced on Åland, giving rise to the name Ålvados. The main ingredient in this is apples, for which the Åland Islands are well-known.

Pontikka and schnapps

The distilling of spirits evidently spread to Scandinavia in the late 15th century and to Finland a little later. A glass or spoonful of the home brew was a

Cramp

2 cl Finlandia Vodka or
Finlandia Cranberry Fusion
2 cl Cranberry liquer

Fill a tall glass with ice cubes. Measure out the vodka or Cranberry Fusion and the cranberry liqueur into it. Add some apple juice and top the glass up with Sprite. Decorate with a slice or segment of lime.

Call of the Crane

Cranberry liquer
Champagne or sparkling wine

Measure out a couple of centilitres of cold cranberry liquer into each champagne glass and fill them up with champagne or sparkling wine. (Float a couple of whole cranberries in each glass.)

Battle tank

2 cl Finlandia Vodka or
Finlandia Cranberry Fusion
2 cl blackcurrant liquer
cranberry juice
ice cubes

Fill an on-the-rocks whisky glass with ice cubes. Measure in the Finlandia Vodka or Cranberry Fusion. Top up with cranberry juice. Decorate with a slice of lime if you like.

good way of keeping diseases and minor complaints at bay and keeping the people happy and the soldiers in fighting condition.

The distilling of spirits at home remained legal until 1866, when it was prohibited by law and replaced with factory-distilled products. It was during the period of total prohibition in 1919–1932 that spirits distilled secretly at home came to be referred to as *pontikka*, "moonshine", the production and sale of which is nowadays subject to licence.

Wherever you may be in Finland, one of the alternatives if you want to order a glass of schnapps will be the clear 38% spirit known officially as *Koskenkorva*, in everyday parlance as *Koskis* and by the pet name of *Kossu*. Having only a moderate alcohol content, it can be drunk as a schnapps just as it is, preferably ice-cold, usually out of a small, clear glass. More exotic schnapps glasses include ones cut out of lumps of ice or hollowed out of a cucumber or potato.

Koskenkorva is made mainly from barley, but with some rye added, and it is colourless and fairly neutral in taste, with a softness which is derived from its low sugar content. It can also be bought ready flavoured with vanilla, wild berries or mint, or if you don't mind the greyish-black colour, with sal ammoniac or tar.

Finlandia Vodka is also distilled from barley, but it has an alcohol content of 40% and is better suited as a base for cocktails and long drinks. This dry, neutral spirit is a popular export item which can be obtained in bars, restaurants, liquor stores and duty-free shops throughout the world.

The usual thing to say when raising your glass is *skål*, although foreign visitors are often taught one of the many more facetious forms such as *kippis*, *terve*, *hei hei*, *tilulilulei*, or even *hölökynkölökyn*, which only a Finn can be expected to pronounce properly!

Sweets, Chocolates and Other Frivolities

The Finns produce excellent chocolates filled with berry or liqueur flavours, and also truffles and jellies. The most beloved and nostalgic of all, however, is Fazer's Blue chocolate, a milk chocolate made by the Fazer Company for a hundred years and always wrapped in blue paper. It comes as individual chocolates and also in bars, even flavoured with chilli if you like. Other irresistible delights for the Finns are liquorice, sal ammoniac and tar pastilles, which people living abroad use to dispel their bouts of homesickness.

Smoke and tar are two utterly Finnish smells. Tar used to be a cure for all manner of ills in the past, and the old saying goes that "If sauna, spirits and tar won't help, then the disease will be the death of you."

Tar was an important commodity in the 19th century, when it was exported for use in shipbuilding, and the smell is a familiar one around boatyards, especially in old rowing boats and fishing boats. The bottoms of the wooden skis that were still in use in the 1960s were also treated with tar.

Nowadays soaps are perfumed with tar, and you can generate an authentic smell in your sauna with a few drops of tar oil. The innovations that arose out

Liquorice, sal ammoniac and tar are a passion for many people, mostly as pastilles, but they can even be found as flavourings for chocolate.

of a recent tar project in Kainuu included tar mustard, tar vinegar and tar jelly. A taste of tar can also be found sometimes in rye bread and certain patisserie products. Tar chocolates are again a delicacy that is largely confined to Kainuu, but the tar-flavoured *Leijona* (Lion) pastilles are a classic. Tar ice cream caused a great sensation even in the more elegant of restaurants when it first came on the market.

This familiar taste has also been added to alcohol to produce tar schnapps and liqueurs, with or without honey. One of the latest Finnish-minded restaurants is now offering tar-flavoured butter to spread on your bread.

The other "black passion" for the Finns is liquorice, the roots of which go back to 18th-century England. The basic ingredients are liquorice extract, liquorice powder, sugar and flour, which are cooked together to produce a black substance that can then be flavoured with linseed or various berries, for example. It is sold in the shape of bars, buttons, ribbons, mats and pipes.

The third place in a vote for the most beloved of all Finnish food products went to sal ammoniac, the salty-sweet taste of which comes from ammonium chloride. The original form in which it was sold as a sweet was the diamond shape familiar from a pack of cards, and its pastilles could only be bought from pharmacists at first.

This very popular flavour can now be found in ice cream and honey, and, as an "adults only" sweet, in *Koskenkorva* spirit. A couple of summers ago a new barbeque speciality came out in the form of pork chops marinaded in sal ammoniac, and the chocolate lover can be consoled by the fact that the flavour has also been combined with white and dark chocolate.

Where the world at large chews spearmint-flavoured xylitol chewing gum, the Finns will often prefer theirs to be sal ammoniac-flavoured.

Tasty Souvenirs

It is fun to remember your trip to Finland over a meal, and one way of doing this is by laying the table Finnish-style. Choose an original Marimekko tablecloth, use tableware that is of Finnish design, or at least take out the most straightforward of your single-coloured plates and bowls. Light some candles and have some Finnish music playing in the background: old tangos, classical works by Sibelius or modern rock 'n roll. This is what the Finns do at a celebration meal. When you raise your glass at the beginning of the meal, wish each other *Hyvää ruokahalua!*, a good appetite, in Finnish.

The food can be quite simple if you wish: some rye bread, crispbread, butter and Finnish cheese.

If you want a plate of special delicacies, try to assemble a mini-*smörgåsbord* on one plate. This could include cured herring, tinned vendace, lightly salted or smoked salmon, smoked reindeer meat and Finnish cheese with rye bread or crispbread and Karelian pasties. End your meal with light-roast coffee served with Finnish berry liqueur and chocolates.

Fazer's Blue is the best-known of the Finnish makes of chocolate.

You can easily take Finnish foods home with you, although if you are travelling by air you must be careful to observe the security regulations. At least at Helsinki Airport, you can buy Finnish foods and drinks after passing through the security check. Travel times are shorter than ever, most foods keep comparatively well, especially if you ask the shop to pack them in readiness for a journey.
If you have a long journey ahead of you it is worth buying preserves, e.g.:

- juices, jams (lingonberry, cloudberry, cranberry and rowanberry) and jellies
- vodka, liqueurs (cranberry, arctic bramble, cloudberry and sea buckthorn)
- bread, ranging from rye bread (which keeps very well) and crispbread to Karelian pasties
- reindeer meat, ham, various sausages (check what you are allowed to take into your own country!)
- herring and Baltic herring preserved in various marinades, also original Finnish fish such as vendace and lampreys in vacuum packs
- sweets, from chocolate to liquorice and pastilles, and
- tar-flavoured syrups and jellies.

The classic fruit jellies are known as *Vihreät kuulat*, Green Balls.

Index

The following modern recipes were created at the Tertti Manor House by chef Ninni Lokonen:

Acknowledgements

Especial thanks are extended to Matti and Pepita Pylkkänen and the staff of Tertti Manor House, particularly the head chef, Ninni Lokonen, who created and arranged the modern manor house dishes.

Thanks also go to my husband Jyri Muttonen, Mirkku Tenhunen, Tuula Kuntz, Seija Lumatjärvi, Seija Kurunmäki and all the people who have influenced the production of this book, also to Pekka Pellinen of Finlandia Vodka Worldwide Ltd, Pirjo Huhtala of Valio, Liisa Hervonen of Raisio, Kirsti Seppälä of Tapola Oy and Kirsi Lauttia of Iittala company.

Sources of photographs

Alko Ltd 209, Finnish Press Agency / Bengt Geijestam 21, Kari Hautala 124, Ari Heinonen 200, Hannu Lindroos 139, Jorma Marstio 16, 154, Norman Ojanen 27, 53, 109, 160, 164, 178, Jukka Pakarinen 62, 110, 180, Seppo Saarentola 29, 163, 172–173, 188, 198–199, Studio Tunturilappi 189, Jouni Törmänen 30, 58, Jarmo Wright 10, 112, 128–129 • Katja Hagelstam 6–7, 13, Pekka Haraste 61, 153, Hannu Hautala 76–77, 106–107, HK Ruokatalo Group Oyj / Timo Viljakainen 194 • Antti Huittinen 8–9, 212, Hannu Huttu 98 centre left, centre right, Asko Hämäläinen 187, Iittala Material Bank 207 • Hanna Immonen 18, 23, 37, 43, 49, 54, 57, 71–73, 79, 81, 84, 89, 93, 103, 105, 119, 121–122, 130, 145, 147–148, 151, 157, 190, 193, 205, 210, Milla von Konow 94, Mauri Korhonen 90–91, 98 top left, top right, Emmi Kyytsönen 213, Lehtikuva Picture Agency 184, Leipätiedotus ry. 170, Leuku Picture Agency / Pekka Antikainen 66, Jorma Luhta endpapers • Pekka Luukkola 2, 32–33, Sebastian Nurmi 177, Mikko Oksanen 65 , Kari Palsila 182, Jorma Peiponen 98 bottom left, bottom right, 101, Sami Repo 35, Mika Rokka 46–47, Anne Saarenoja 40, 86, 133, 136, 144, 217, Juhani Seppovaara 203, Tiina Somerpuro 143, Tapola Oy 197, Vaasan & Vaasan Group 141, 175, Valio Ltd 22

Rowanberry, pihlajanmarja, *Sorbus aucuparia*.

Weights

1 pound (lb) = 16 ounces = 453,6 grams (g)

1 ounce (oz) = 28,35 g

1 kilogram (kg) = 1000 g = 2 lbs 3 oz

100 g = 3,5 oz

Measures

1 US gallon = 4 liquid quarts = 3,785 liters (l)

1 liquid quart = 2 liquid pints = 9,5 deciliters (dl)

1 liquid pint = 16 US fl oz = 4, 73 dl

1 cup = 8 US oz = 2,37 dl

1 US fluid ounce (US fl oz) = 29,6 milliliters (ml)

1 quart (dry) = 1,1 l

1 liter = 10 dl = (more than) 2 pints

1 deciliter = (less than) 1/2 cup

Temperatures

Fahrenheit	*Celsius*
268°F	131°C
350°F	177°C
375–400°F	190–204°C
450–500°F	232–260°C

Celsius	*Fahrenheit*
100°C	212°F
200°C	392°F
250°C	482°F
300°C	572°F